NOTES FOR THE
JOURNEY
WITHIN

**Essentials
of the Art
of Living**

GURUDEV
SRI SRI RAVI SHANKAR

GREENLEAF
BOOK GROUP PRESS

Published by Greenleaf Book Group Press
Austin, Texas
www.gbgpress.com

Distributed by Greenleaf Book Group

For ordering information or special discounts for bulk purchases, please contact Greenleaf Book Group at PO Box 91869, Austin, TX 78709, 512.891.6100.

Design and composition by Greenleaf Book Group and Kim Lance
Cover design by Greenleaf Book Group and Kim Lance

Publisher's Cataloging-in-Publication data is available.

Print ISBN: 979-8-88645-067-5

eBook ISBN: 979-8-88645-068-2

Since 1981, the Art of Living Foundation has helped millions of people to relieve stress and anxiety through breathwork and meditation.

To offset the number of trees consumed in the printing of our books, Greenleaf donates a portion of the proceeds from each printing to the Arbor Day Foundation. Greenleaf Book Group has replaced over 50,000 trees since 2007.

Printed in the United States of America on acid-free paper

23 24 25 26 27 28 29 30   10 9 8 7 6 5 4 3 2 1

First Edition

Contents

1   BASIC PRINCIPLES OF THE ART OF LIVING

PART TWO:
STARTING WHERE YOU ARE   **17**

 NAVIGATING STRESS AND CHALLENGES

3   RELATIONSHIPS: FRIENDS, FAMILY, AND THE PEOPLE IN YOUR LIFE

4 ACTING IN THE WORLD: HOW TO HANDLE LIFE'S EVENTS AND SITUATIONS

5   CHASING HAPPINESS: THE NATURE OF DESIRES

6 THE SENSES

PART THREE: MOVING FROM THE SMALL SELF TO THE BIG SELF AND BEYOND

7 UNDERSTANDING YOUR MIND

8 MEDITATION

9 SERVICE: GIVING BACK AND MAKING A DIFFERENCE

10 THE SPIRITUAL PATH: EXPANDING YOUR AWARENESS

11 THE SPIRITUAL TEACHER

12 YOUR HIGHER SELF: THE DIVINE IN YOU

13   ONENESS/GOD/THE DIVINE

Before You Start . . .

Spiritual teacher and humanitarian Gurudev Sri Sri Ravi Shankar has changed the lives of millions of people around the world for the better. Yet many in the West have not been introduced to his profound and practical approach to living a spiritual life. This book is meant to bridge that gap.

Gurudev's teachings are twofold. On one hand, he shares his insights on the art of living through his many talks, books, and online videos. His approach to lasting well-being—rather than chasing happiness or retreating from the stresses of life—is about finding balance, peace, and even joy, amid the ups and downs we face every day.

Then, to complement these insights, Gurudev offers effective mind/body techniques to make those principles second nature, not simply something to understand intellectually.

Still, even just reading or hearing his teachings can make a huge difference in how you live your life, how you interact with your family, friends, and coworkers, how you understand the spiritual path, and how you walk it yourself.

• • • • •

Gurudev founded the Art of Living Foundation in 1981 and has been teaching SKY Breath Meditation, a unique meditation technique for health and mental wellness, for more than forty years.

In June of 1995, Gurudev began a weekly tradition of creating a short talk, often on a subject that was relevant to current events or in response to questions posed by audiences at his events as he went from country to country speaking and teaching. What resulted were powerful words of wisdom, accompanied by much celebration, laughter, and lightheartedness.

Gurudev's talks were then transcribed, and these "knowledge sheets" were sent by fax to Art of Living groups on every continent to read at their weekly meetings when they sat to do their practice together.

Later, a weekly "News Flash" was added to chronicle the highlights of Gurudev's extensive travels—from meetings with heads of state and important religious figures to his students' extraordinary experiences, as well as humorous moments on the road.

This book is a compilation of many of those knowledge sheets written between June 1995 to 2002, plus excerpts from other talks on various topics he's given over the years.

For those who may be new to his teachings, there's a section in the beginning of the book called Foundations, which will serve as an introduction to some of the main principles that characterize his approach to life—and living artfully.

That being said, the book can be read from front to back or simply by choosing notes that speak to you on a given day.

May this collection of insights help you on your journey within, to that all-encompassing love, joy, and peace at your core!

—The editors

PART
1

FOUNDATIONS

Basic Principles of the Art of Living

1. BALANCING UPS AND DOWNS

Life is a play of opposites. Sometimes there's failure, and sometimes you meet with success; at times there's gain and at other times loss; sometimes there's happiness and sometimes pain. These come and go.

When you get something you want, you soar to the ceiling; when you lose something, you fall hard. This isn't advisable. If from within, we lose our balance, our centeredness, we won't be able to move forward in life. So wisdom is keeping the equanimity, the balance in life.

When you accept that contrasting experiences enrich each other, life is less stressful. Opposite values simply coexist on this planet.

Creation, destruction.

Joy, suffering.

Pleasure, pain.

But know that you are something beyond that. This understanding is a gift given to the world from the ancient Indian philosophy, the *Vedas*.

Ultimately, life is bigger than the pairs of opposites. The world is full of paradoxes and life is full of opposites. The art is to embrace the opposites, accommodate the paradoxes, and live with a smile.

2. NATURE OF THE MIND: HOLDING ON TO THE NEGATIVE

Reflect on whether you're holding on to the positive or the negative.

Actually, life has so much that is positive. Life is made up of 80 percent positivity and only 20 percent negativity, that which causes problems. But we make this 20 percent into 200 percent!

In every life, some good has happened, but the nature of the mind is that it ignores the positive and clings to the negative. And this is what disturbs us.

Observe the nature of mind. If you're given ten compliments and one insult, what does your mind hang on to? That one insult.

You say, "Everything is fine, but . . ." We use this quite often: "He's a nice guy, but . . ." We put a break there. Be aware of this tendency. Whenever we say "but," we can just be aware and say to ourselves, "I'm saying 'but'!" Having this awareness makes you very natural, simple, and open from inside.

The most precious thing in life is to maintain the innocence that we have. We're born with some innocence in us. As we become more and more intelligent, we tend to lose innocence. We become a little more stiff. Dropping the stiffness, we find life is much more rewarding, enjoyable, and interesting.

So when we know this, we're already one step out of it. Time and again, we must realize "I am going on a negative trip" and immediately come back to the here and now.

However, when you culture your mind with meditation, its tendency of holding on to negative emotions starts to drop. The mind becomes purer and purer and begins to reflect its true nature, that of acceptance, support, and love.

3. CHALLENGES MAKE YOU STRONGER

Most people wish for a problem-free life. However, such a life, if it were even possible, would be dull and boring. As humans we are shaped by both positive and not-so-positive experiences. Challenging circumstances push people to expand their limits and bring more richness and beauty to the human experience.

If one doesn't have any problems, that person is likely to end up becoming a problem for others! It's better to *have* a problem than *be* a problem.

It's through challenges and failures that we develop our skills and strengths. Look back and reflect on the many times you've failed. Don't you now feel that those failures were good for you? When you look back at your failures and challenges, you'll see that you have learned something from them, and that they've been stepping-stones for you to move ahead.

For example, a tough boss will bring out your skills and abilities and help your capabilities to grow. You can either get frustrated with that boss, or you can see that they're providing abundant opportunities to develop skills that will last a lifetime. However, for that to happen, you'll need to shift your perspective.

For instance, if your boss is disorganized—rather than complain—help your boss to get organized. If your boss is habitually critical of you, practice the art of taking criticism from a rational point of view and commit to self-improvement rather than move toward dejection.

Know that every experience adds dimension, depth, and richness to your life. An example of this is rest and activity. Rest and activity are opposite values, but they complement each other. The deeper you're able to rest, the more dynamic you'll be in activity.

4. A DREAM WITHIN A DREAM

What happened yesterday? You may have been happy or sad. Maybe you argued, talked, danced, laughed, and cried. Is it here now? Can you hold on to that now?

What happened a month ago? Two months ago? What were you like two years ago? Up until this very moment, isn't it all like a dream? Could this be a dream? You'll go to bed today, and then tomorrow something will happen. The day will end, and the next day something else will happen and end. And so on for another ten days, a month, two months, six months—isn't it like a dream? Isn't it like a movie?

Events pass, but they give you an impression that they're permanent. The camera in your mind creates the illusion that they'll stay and they're huge.

What is it that you're hanging on to? Your wants, likes, and dislikes. What is it you dislike and what is it you crave? Where are they? Are they not just fleeting impressions in the mind, coming and vanishing, coming and vanishing?

Those moments stay in the photographic mind and rob you of clarity. You become unable to see anything else clearly. When you're thinking about what happened the previous day, your mind isn't alert and awake. You're unable to perceive things right now.

In photography, when several pictures are taken on the same piece of film, it looks very funny. You may take a picture of a bird and then of someone else. In the photograph, you'll see the bird sitting on someone's nose—it's a double exposure. We aren't just double exposing our minds. We're doing multiple exposures.

Wake up and see that all of it has been like a dream and is finished. It's not here right now. Then where are your cravings?

When you can see this whole flow of events as fleeting happenings and remain untouched by them, you're happy. Joy springs out of you like a fountain. Every event becomes a game, a celebration.

5. THREE TYPES OF LISTENING

There are three types of listening.

One is hearing through your intellect. You may be reading this while constantly inside you something is happening, where you're saying, "Yes, yes. What he is saying is right." You keep accepting certain things, things that you already know.

And you resist those things that you don't know. You say, "No, how could this be? How can that be the case? No." You don't let those ideas in but keep them out. In this situation, there's no need to listen because you are only listening to those things that you already know.

The second type of listening is emotional listening. This is how you listen to music, where nothing really goes in. You simply listen and let go. Of course, you absorb everything, but you don't retain anything. Neither of these types of listening is complete. In fact, you can't call either of them listening. It's hearing.

The third type of listening is a beautiful blend of these two. You hear with a willingness to listen and at the same time, you're asking questions too. Those questions that come from this type of listening are sincere questions.

The most important thing is to become aware of what's happening in the mind and observe how we listen.

6. RESISTANCE

To gain peace of mind, embrace the disturbance. Say, "All right, I'll be disturbed for a while now." Why? Because observation reduces the disturbance.

If you resist stress, it persists. The moment you embrace it, it dissolves and disappears. When you stop resisting the storms of life and start accepting them with open arms, they'll subside on their own. That's the purpose of all spiritual practices like meditation.

Don't be in a hurry to get rid of the storms—be with them. Looking for perfection creates imperfection inside you. If you're peaceful, everything around you becomes peaceful.

You are the center of this universe. Wherever you go, you carry your own mind, and wherever you go, you'll create your own storms. It may appear to be calm and quiet for some time, but the storm will surface sooner or later. Unless you realize this, nothing will hold. There is no other permanent solution. Don't resist the storms; instead, see them as an amazing play of your personality.

7. EXPECTATIONS REDUCE JOY

Expectations are just imaginations of the future. They're your imaginations of what reality could be, but reality may not live up to your imagination. If you expect something, inevitably you'll be disappointed or the joy you'll get out of it will be reduced.

For example, your friends have been raving about a certain film. You get all excited to see this movie, and you build up your expectations. When you finally watch the movie, it's a big letdown. It doesn't measure up to your expectations. But if you hadn't heard anything about the same film and had just gone on the spur of the moment with a friend, you'd probably have enjoyed it twice as much.

Someone tells you about some exotic fruit that grows in Thailand. They describe the taste, the color, the smell, until you can't wait to try this wonderful fruit. Sometime later, your friend gets a hold of this fruit and brings you some with great excitement. When you actually taste it, you find it's too sweet or too sour or you don't like the texture. You're disappointed and so is your friend who expected you to think it's fantastic.

Think back to the times you had high expectations and things didn't work the way you'd hoped. Remember how let down you felt.

Now think of a time when something good happened when you least expected it. Remember the joy you felt.

Can you let your expectations go . . . right *now*?

8. DON'T BE A FOOTBALL OF OTHER PEOPLE'S OPINIONS

You forget one thing: People's likes and dislikes are like bubbles or ripples on the surface of water. Why do you give so much importance to thoughts? One minute the thought is there; the next minute it's not. Everything is changing. In this changing world, what changes most are thoughts. It's like trying to hold on to a wave that is disappearing.

Someone may think that you're such a nice person. How long does it take for this to change? You may do good things and people criticize you. Someone may even do horrible things and be admired. So why base your life on someone else's opinion?

Wake up. Let anybody have an opinion. Let them. You move on. It appears to be tough, but once you take this step, it's not so tough. Opinions of people come and go. They think bad about you; then they think good about you. All this happens. So, in any situation, it isn't worth wasting your time on what those people are thinking about you.

The main thing is, don't be a football of other people's opinions. Many times, you do things because others want you to do it. No need! Be strong in yourself and see life from a bigger perspective.

9. DISPASSION IS LETTING GO

Every night, when your head hits the pillow, what do you do? You simply let go. You let sleep take over.

Breathe in. How long can you hold that? At some point, you have to let go. So, while passion is like breathing in, dispassion is like breathing out. We have to let go. Unless you have dispassion, passion will turn into depression.

Dispassion may appear to be a very big, philosophical thing: "Oh well, to be dispassionate means maybe I have to become a recluse and go to the Himalayas, with a necklace of holy beads." No, it's an inherent quality in human life to let go. After you've heard or seen something, if you're unable to let go of it, do you know what that state is called? Trauma.

Traumas are those experiences that your mind catches on to and is unable to let go. So, in some sense, we're traumatized to varying degrees.

If you're traumatized, you can never feel passion or dispassion, compassion or love. Your trauma puts a block to all these qualities. So, see life from a bigger context. At the end of the day, the curtain is going to fall, and the show will be finished. We must be aware of this.

10. THE MIND WANTS ENDLESS JOY

People who are single think they'll be happy if they get married.

Married people think they were better off when they were single.

There's a deep desire for some joy in the future: If I change my town, I will be happy. If I change my relationship, or my job, or my company, I will be happier.

A child thinks that when he or she grows up and goes to college, he or she will be happy. A college student says, "Once I get a job, I'll be happy." A manager says, "When I become the director, I'll be happy." Postponing happiness to sometime in the future can make you miserable right now.

Pleasure can also tire you. How long can you look at something beautiful? Eventually, you'll get tired of it; your eyelids will shut. How long can you smell a beautiful fragrance? People working in the perfume factories are sick of perfumes. If you like donuts, how many can you stuff in your mouth? How much ice cream can you enjoy? How much music can you hear? For how long can you enjoy touching and being touched?

The world is full of pleasure for the five senses, but the senses have their limitations. Still, the mind wants endless joy. An attitude of "So what! Let it be, whatever," takes away the feverishness in you and brings you to that state of dispassion, or centeredness.

Dispassion is NOT apathy! Often, we think dispassion means being unenthusiastic, depressed, and not interested in anything. This is not dispassion!

Dispassion is the lack of feverishness. Dispassion is full of activity and enthusiasm, yet devoid of feverishness. Dispassion toward the enjoyment of the five senses or spiritual enjoyment, the outer world or the inner world, is one of the foundations of wisdom.

Dispassion is the only way you can be centered. There's no other way.

11. THE PURPOSE OF ALL CHANGE IS TO "POLISH" YOU

Everything is transitory. Everything changes. Nobody is all bad. People get into different moods. Their moods change, and their behaviors change. Their likes and dislikes change. Your likes and dislikes change. Your way of looking at things changes. Events change. No event stays and remains the same. So, everything is changing.

The purpose of it all is to polish you. You're polished in joy, and you're polished in sorrow. You're polished in this event and in that event. So, everything in the world polishes you.

Just move lightly. Move above the events, knowing they're all there to polish you, to refine you, and they don't have any real attraction or juice. They're like the straw that's left when the sugarcane is crushed. Fiber comes out on the other side, but all the juice is removed. It's only good as fuel. If you know this, you're able to drop the events. When you think that you'll get some juice out of straw, you'll go on crushing it.

Once you know there's no juice in it and that it's just straw, there's no effort required to drop it. It drops off you. When you wake up after having a dream, you don't say that you'll renounce it or drop it. You don't make an effort to drop it. Once you wake up, the dream is gone.

Wake up and see! What is this world? Is there any juice in it? There is no juice!

12. LIVE IN THE PRESENT MOMENT

Live in the present moment. *Be* in the moment. We often dwell in the past, worrying about what someone did ten years ago, holding a grudge against them . . . "Oh, my friend said this thing to me ten years ago. I will never speak to him again." Have you seen how foolishly we make such resolutions?

Have you observed what is happening in your mind every moment? It vacillates between the past and the future. It's either in the past, occupied with what's happened, or in the future thinking about what you have to do.

Knowledge is being aware of this phenomenon of the mind—of what is happening right now in your mind as you are reading this. Information can be acquired by reading books or browsing the internet, but the experience of being aware of your own mind is different.

It's only possible to grasp the reality of the present moment totally when you see everything that's happened in the past as a dream. When you let go of everything that's happened until now as a dream, only then can you understand the truth of the present moment.

13. TRYING AND DOING

Someone calls you on the phone and asks you to come to dinner, and you say, "I'll try to come." This usually means you have more or less decided not to go. Trying implies a half-hearted action with a sense of failure or inability built into it. The action lacks 100 percent attention. Trying is a strain in the mind. It means there is some inner resistance there.

Children don't *try* to do anything. They just do it. Doing means putting your 100 percent into it. Say a child wants to move a big chair. He will push and push, putting 100 percent into it. Then there's no regret if it doesn't work out since he has done his best.

14. ACCEPT PEOPLE AND SITUATIONS AS THEY ARE

Accept people as they are. You can't expect everyone to be just like you or to agree with you. The world is so diverse. People are so diverse.

If you were to meet someone who was just like you, I tell you, you wouldn't be able to stand them for five minutes. But unconsciously, we want everyone to be like us, and how many problems does this create for others?

So, accept people and situations as they are without expecting everybody to agree with what we think is right. Give people time and space to grow.

15. DON'T SEE INTENTIONS BEHIND OTHER PEOPLE'S MISTAKES

Everybody makes mistakes. And when it happens to you, what do you do? You make excuses, saying, "Oh, everybody makes mistakes," or "I didn't do anything wrong." But when somebody else does it, what do we say? "That guy intentionally did this!"

Say you're walking into somebody's house and the wind blows the door shut after you. And someone behind you thinks, "See! I was going in, and this person slammed the door in my face!" And you may not even be aware this has happened. We see intention behind others' mistakes, and we suffer a lot.

Be generous. Be magnanimous and accommodate them. Forgive and forget. Can we do that? When we do that, we gain more friends. Your life becomes easier. Your mind becomes calmer.

16. LET PEOPLE HAVE THEIR OPINIONS

Don't worry about what others are thinking about you. Give them the freedom of thinking. Let anyone think whatever they want to think about you.

The secret is, nobody has time to think about you. Everyone is caught up in their own world. If they're really enlightened or a very wise person, then they may think about you, but not everybody will be thinking about you.

There are people who think about you—your parents, your partner, and your children—but you don't worry about what their opinions are. You worry about the opinion of someone who doesn't give you any thought. You worry about your neighbors' opinions. And they're caught up in their own things. So, let people have their opinions.

17. ACT WITHOUT ANXIETY ABOUT THE RESULT

When we perform every action with an eye on the end result, we get lost in the goal and don't enjoy the means of getting there. But when we perform actions as an expression of joy and don't bother about the result, the action itself brings fulfillment.

When we act expecting joy, the action becomes inferior. For example, you want to spread happiness, but if you try to find out whether the people around you have become happy, you get entangled and less effective. In the process, you lose your happiness!

Anxiety about the outcome of your action is what pulls you down. If you start worrying at the beginning of a project, then your whole enthusiasm for the project gets dampened. When you're aware of your potential, just jump into action without bothering about the result. One who isn't concerned about the outcome and is centered on the action goes beyond conflicts and the dualities of success and failure.

The wise one is beyond all actions yet continues to engage in action. Keep doing your work and drop the expectation for the result.

The result serves as the motivation for you to start acting. When you're bogged down by laziness, you need motivation to do something, and the expected fruit of action acts as the motivating factor.

But once you start acting, let go of the expected result. Just focus on the work at hand. This is the way of the wise!

18. STRETCH OUT YOUR HAND FIRST

Everyone has had some problem with someone. You've shouted at them, or something happened and afterward you expected to patch things up. Yet you expect the other person to come forward.

Suppose you want to greet them, but you have one concern: *If I put myself out there, and they don't respond, what will happen to me?* Suppose you stretch out your hand, and they don't shake your hand. What happens? You feel embarrassed and hurt. The greatest fear in the world is getting hurt. We don't mind physical hurt so much as getting hurt mentally and emotionally, a bruised ego.

If everybody thinks, *Let the other person come and reach out first*, then who will come? Nobody. This is what prevents people from coming together and from feeling this sense of belongingness.

Take a stand and stretch out your hand first. If the other person doesn't shake it, fine. So what? In fact, everybody wants to shake hands. They want to reach out, but they're afraid, waiting for somebody else to take the initiative and do it first.

19. NATURALNESS

Do you feel at home when you're a guest at someone else's house? Do you feel uneasy? Afraid to collapse into the couch if you're tired?

Now, how do you want your guests to feel when they're in your home? Do you want them to be uneasy and very formal? Don't you want them to make themselves at home, comfortable? Yet we don't make ourselves at home at someone else's house.

How expanded a personality do you have? This can be measured by one simple thing: how at home you feel in situations.

If you take a boy of fifteen and put him in a group of people who are sixty to seventy, does he feel right at home? Not at all. He feels totally out of place and wants to run back to his friends.

When we start supporting one another and supporting one another's enthusiasm, we take interest, and we feel at home in any situation.

That is exactly where our personality grows and expands, with this feeling of being at home with everybody, with every age group. If you can be one with all life situations, you can be one with the entire universe. This makes the expansion of total consciousness possible.

This is the state of naturalness, feeling at home wherever you are. This is the nature of your being.

So, when you feel out of place, just be aware of how you're feeling. Your awareness of it will allow that feeling to fade, allowing your naturalness to come out.

20. THE VASTNESS OF LIFE

Life is not just the time between some events, the time between birth and death. Life is beyond that.

Life is an eternal continuum. Don't measure life by events or feelings. Life goes beyond the years. Life is so big—too big to be contained by time or space. If you realize this, just this awareness takes you beyond the little mind. When you see how big and vast life is, then fears, concerns, sorrow, sadness . . . they all disappear.

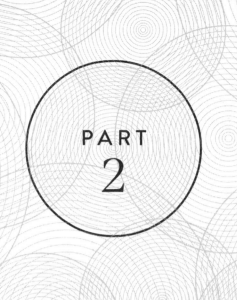

PART
2

STARTING

WHERE YOU ARE

Navigating Stress and Challenges

1. OVERCOMING EVENTS

DECEMBER 14, 1995

BANGALORE ASHRAM, INDIA

All the problems that you face in life are because you attach over-importance to events. The events grow bigger, while you remain smaller.

Say, for example, you're riding a motorcycle on a busy street, and in front of you, another vehicle is emitting exhaust fumes. You have three options:

1. You can complain, somehow bear with it, and still follow the vehicle.

2. You can slow down or pull over for a while to allow the vehicle to move far away from you.

3. You can use your skill, overtake the vehicle, and forget about it.

Most of you get stuck in the events and, as in the first option, are miserable, "inhaling fumes" throughout your journey.

The second option isn't much better. You don't get permanent relief because another bigger vehicle might come in front of you. Running away from events is not the permanent solution.

Wise people use their skill to surmount the event. When the vehicle (you) is in perfect condition, the skill is most effective.

You condition yourself through *sadhana* (spiritual practices). And being with a spiritual teacher enhances your skill.

> *If you've gotten stuck in events before now, don't worry, the mistakes you've made in the past have made you humble—not that you need to make mistakes in the future to become humble.* (Laughter)

2. YOU ARE UNBREAKABLE

When everything falls apart, if you can stand up and laugh, then you've lived a life. Otherwise, you have simply existed like a machine. Laughter is most needed when the world comes caving in. Stand up and laugh. Then you have seen life in its vastness.

Imagine a big river is flowing, and at one particular point, there's a stone. The water splashes against the stone, trying to pass over it. When the water hits the stone, does anything happen to the water? Does it break?

Similarly, all the events cannot break the spirit in you. Even events that appear to be insurmountable cannot break the spirit because life moves on. Just like the water flows on, in the same way the current of life is a continuum. It may appear blocked here or stagnant there, but it's just an appearance. It's not the reality.

3. THE "IT'S NOT OKAY" SEED

OCTOBER 21, 1998

MONTREAL ASHRAM, CANADA

Most of us come into this world with the seed "It's not okay" in us. And all our life, we try to correct events, people, and situations. But how much can you correct? It's like trying to rearrange the clouds in the sky.

This seed doesn't allow you to be happy, to smile from your heart, to be loving, and be lovable; it's there all the time like a thorn—irritating, irritating.

This seed—"It's not okay"—brings you back into this world again and again.

How do you burn this seed?

1. First, recognize that it's there; this can happen in deep introspection and meditation.

2. Sometimes, you feel your body, mind, intellect, memory, and ego are also not okay. These are also part of the world. Acknowledge what you see as an imperfection and offer it to the Divine.

3. Have faith in the infinite organizing power of Universal Intelligence and have the sincere feeling, "Let Thy will be done." Then the seed—"It's not okay"—gets burned.

"Thy will be done" is a state of total contentment, a state of just love. We don't even need to make it a statement about the future: "Thy will alone is happening now."

> *Question*: So, everything that happens is God's will?
>
> *Gurudev*: Yes, including the thought, *This shouldn't be happening*.

NEWS FLASH:

One evening this week, Gurudev took a very long walk through the forest after dark. For the flock of students following him, the experience seemed to be a metaphor for the spiritual path: trusting and following the spiritual teacher along a steep and narrow trail through the pitch-black darkness, without any idea of how to find their way, yet laughing merrily anyway.

We are happy to report that Art of Living courses have now begun in El Salvador and Zimbabwe.

4. EMOTIONAL TURMOIL

Often, life is caught up in storms. And you aren't yourself when you're in a storm. You don't know what to do. At those moments, all your practices, concepts, ideas, and ideals fall apart. Even when the storm has subsided, the very memory of it disturbs you.

This is the only basic problem in the universe. You can attach it to a thousand reasons, but the problem is how to free your life from the storm that has gripped it.

The first thing to do is to become aware of this. At that moment, the storm will subside.

Next, stop regretting things. It's Nature. Waves come, and for no reason there is turmoil in the mind. There can't be an ocean without waves.

Every event touches life somewhere on its surface. Take all that comes with both your hands. Don't say that it's not possible for you. This thought of something being not possible means that you're resisting. This makes the storms stay for long periods.

Stand there with your arms open. Say, "Whatever storms come, let them." You grow out of them. You become bigger. Have this faith that come what may, there is nothing that can destroy me. It may be excruciatingly painful, but it doesn't matter. It still can't destroy or kill me. I am here. I am much, much bigger than all these emotions, commotions, or waves. They all rise inside me, in me, and in no way can they destroy me. Let them be.

Pleasant sensations arise, and unpleasant sensations arise. Good feelings arise, and painful feelings arise. See the broader perspective of one's Self. Otherwise, we keep running away from small things.

5. WORRY AND THOUGHT

When a thought arises in the mind, it isn't easy to get rid of it. The thought keeps coming back over and over again, and if you decide to do something else, you'll feel uneasy until you finish with that thought. It becomes irritating, like a grain of sand in the eye.

Similarly, if you are unhappy about something, that sadness doesn't easily leave you, whatever you do to get rid of it.

Streams of thoughts are always passing through the mind. They come and they go. But you may catch hold of one of these thoughts and not allow it to go easily. When one thought is stuck in your mind, like a needle stuck in the groove of an old record, that's worry. And worry causes sorrow. Sorrow comes from getting stuck in one thought or one desire.

Let the thoughts go. Feel that they're not yours. Sorrow disappears as one progresses on the path of knowledge. Yoga and meditation remove sorrow from life and bring joy.

6. PROBLEMS AND SOLUTIONS

NOVEMBER 23, 2000

EUROPEAN ASHRAM, GERMANY

Whenever there's a problem, we either deny it by saying there's no problem, or we call a meeting to solve the problem and make it a big issue. Neither of these helps.

A problem doesn't disappear when you deny it. And it doesn't get solved when you sit to solve it. Most of the meetings to solve problems cause more confusion!

The five steps to solve a problem are:

- Acknowledge the problem; it's there.

- See it as a small problem. Don't say it's big.

- If it concerns other people, keep in touch with them instead of avoiding them.

- Talk less and give time a chance.

- Get together and celebrate. When you celebrate and put the problem on the back burner, you'll see that the problem gets solved in time.

If you don't have any problems, you'll create problems for others! (*Laughter*)

If you have a small problem in your pocket to solve, it will give focus to your mind. It's better to *have* a problem than to *be* a problem.

NEWS FLASH:

In New Delhi, the Imam Maulana Ilyasi, who is the founder of the All India Organization of Imams of Mosques, met with Gurudev, along with the Turkish delegation, and participated in a satsang.[1]

Back in Bangalore, Gurudev gave the concluding address at the Confederation of Indian Industry. Participants were stunned when an aggressive heckler was transformed into another joyful participant.

---

1   A gathering that typically includes singing, meditation, and discussion of spiritual topics.

7. PROBLEMS?

AUGUST 24, 2000

EUROPEAN ASHRAM, GERMANY

The first solution to a problem is not to have the problem at all. (*Laughter*)

The second solution is to willingly accept the problem and see it as a challenge.

The third solution is to know that the problem is a boogeyman; it's not real.

The fourth solution is to know that Nature has provided you with the solution even before giving you the problem.

In the spring, the herbs to treat bug bites come first and then the bugs. In the summer, the shade comes before the summer sun gets strong. So, Nature takes good care of you.

8. HANDLING DIFFICULT EMOTIONS

There's a strange relationship between thoughts and feelings. Thoughts provoke feelings, and feelings, in turn, can bring about thoughts.

Feeling is subtler than thinking. Feelings change. You can't have the same feeling all the time. When we feel high, there's no problem. The problem comes when we feel low. Then the more one tries to feel high, the more the low feelings persist.

Have you ever loved your low feelings? You have always fought with them. Just close your eyes and go into the low. Don't do anything; just agree. You'll start rising up in no time. If you try to fight with your feelings, they take a longer time to clear.

People tend to get angry, then sad, and then angry again. People go through the cycle of emotions without awareness. Children also get angry and then cry. However, they snap out of emotions easily. Even before their tears have dried, they start giggling. But adults take months, sometimes even years, to overcome emotions. What prevents adults from snapping out of this cycle and living in the present moment? It is because our emotions are stored at certain points in our body. An event is just a trigger for these emotions to come into play.

Pay attention to the effect of emotions on your body. Every emotion has a corresponding sensation in the body. This phenomenon is connected with the endocrine glands.

In the same way the body influences the mind, the mind can also influence the body. Start observing the sensation in your body that the emotion creates. You'll notice that as you observe the sensation, the emotion starts to dissolve.

Through meditation, we can get centered. This doesn't mean that you become stiff and emotionless, but that emotions don't rule you. Amid a storm of emotions, be solid like a rock—don't let emotions carry you away. Depression and low feelings can't touch you at your core.

However big the clouds are, they can't overshadow the sun. Even on the darkest day, it is still day—clouds can never make it night.

9. DEALING WITH DOUBT

JULY 20, 1995
MONTREAL ASHRAM, CANADA

Doubt is a gray area—neither white nor black. So, how do you resolve a doubt? Accept a doubt as either white or black.

See your doubt as white, and there is no doubt.

See the doubt as black and accept it.

Either way, you accept it and move on.

See someone as either honest or dishonest and accept him. Then your mind becomes quiet, and you are not in the gray area of doubt. Have the conviction, "He is dishonest, and yet he is still part of me. I accept him as he is." That's it. Finished.

Doubt is an unstable state with footing neither on this shore nor on the other. This leads to tension. One way or the other, take a direction and regain your footing.

Have you noticed that you usually doubt the things that are positive in your life? You don't doubt negative things as much. You doubt a person's honesty, and you believe in their dishonesty. When someone is angry with you, you don't doubt their anger. But when someone says they love you, a doubt creeps in: "Do they *really* love me?"

When you're depressed, do you ever think, "Am I *really* depressed?" No, you take your depression as a fact. Yet when you are happy, you doubt: "Am I really happy? Is this really what I wanted?"

You doubt your capability but not your weakness.

Notice this tendency in you to doubt the positive things in your life.
Put doubt in its proper place and doubt the doubts.
Doubt the negative and put your trust in the positive.

10. FIND COMFORT IN CONFLICTS

AUGUST 16, 1995
ROTTERDAM, NETHERLANDS

Conflict is the nature of the world; comfort is the nature of your Higher Self. Amidst conflict, find the comfort.

When you're tired of conflicts and the games of the world, get into the comforts of the Self. When you're bored with comfort, get into the games of the world. If you're on the spiritual path, you can do both simultaneously.

People who love peace don't want conflict, and those who fight don't have peace. What's needed is to be peaceful within and then fight.

Just trying to end a conflict only prolongs it. Instead, face the conflict while seeking the comfort of the Self.

Does this ring a bell? This is the whole message of the *Bhagavad Gita*—Krishna tells Arjuna to be centered in peace and to fight at the same time.

God is alive in the world and has been putting up with all the conflicts in the world throughout the ages. So can you. The moment you agree to be with a conflict, it no longer appears as a conflict to you.

What's more, the nature of this world is that once you resolve one conflict, another arises. For example, a problem with Russia is solved, and then Bosnia is in trouble. You get a cold; then you get better. Your back hurts; then it gets better. And when your body is fine, then the mind goes. Things in this world run this way, don't they?

Misunderstandings simply happen without any intention, and conflicts arise. It's not up to you to resolve them all. Just be with them and be alive!

11. BLAME AND MISERY

MARCH 26, 1996
BANGALORE ASHRAM, INDIA

When a worldly man is miserable, he blames the people around him, the system, and the world in general.

When a seeker, a person seeking spiritual growth, is miserable, he blames not only the world but also the path he's on, the knowledge he's learning, and himself.

It would appear that it's better not to be a seeker so you blame less. But a seeker also enjoys everything much more. There is more love in life and more pain. When there is more joy, the contrast is greater.

> *A certain level of maturity is needed to see things as they are and not blame the path, the self, or the world.*

Do you see what I'm saying?

If one jumps across this chasm of blame and misery, then there is no fall. It is like a quantum leap.

Then why is there misery? It is to develop resilience, forbearance in you. And forbearance can be increased by letting go—and by things that vigorously challenge your patience!

12. ACCEPT THE WORLD AT ITS WORST

JANUARY 22, 1997
DALLAS, TEXAS, UNITED STATES

Suppose the worst of the world is given to you; what would you do with it?

Don't complain if you get the worst. Only complain if you don't get the worst, because if the world is at its worst, then it can only get better, and you are here to make it better.

What happens when you have to make things better all by yourself—when no one comes to help? There are three options:

1. Get frustrated and complain.

2. Thank others for not helping so you can take all the credit for doing it yourself.

3. Be grateful, pray deeply, and know that you'll get all the energy needed to do it alone. There is only one energy in the universe— one Higher Power—that does everything.

NEWS FLASH:

Gurudev made a lightning visit to Dominica—where the cabinet minister for Education and Social Welfare had organized a program—then whisked off to the Caribbean island of St. Lucia.

A diplomatic reception on the island of Curacao (near Venezuela) preceded a public satsang that was filled to capacity. Courses are being organized in various parts of Central and South America.

This trip gave a huge boost to Art of Living activities here. Gurudev and his teachings are now becoming known throughout the Caribbean and Central America.

13. SHARE YOUR JOY

FEBRUARY 26, 1997

HONOLULU, HAWAII, UNITED STATES

Share your joy with everybody.

When you don't share your joy, it reduces.

Share your problems only with the wise, not with any Tom, Dick, or Harry—that just increases the problem.

> *Question*: Gurudev, how do you help people who come to share misery with you?
>
> *Gurudev*: I have a 1,001 ways to help. Often it happens that when they share their problem with me, it's immediately resolved. Other times it requires some patience. Just know that all problems will be taken care of.

Question: How can we help people who share their misery with us?

Gurudev: Listen to others, yet don't listen. Don't take it in too fully. Because if your mind gets stuck there, then not only are they miserable; you also become miserable. Be caring and share spiritual knowledge with them.

NEWS FLASH:

Gurudev outlined a new course for teenagers to help them manage their emotions and thrive on all levels.

The governor of Hawaii and the mayor of Honolulu each wrote letters to Gurudev that expressed their appreciation for his work in Hawaii. A final talk at a hotel in Honolulu rounded out Gurudev's Hawaiian tour.

14. EXPAND YOUR VICES

APRIL 3, 1997
RISHIKESH, INDIA

If you cannot get rid of vices, increase them! Give them a bigger dimension and a different direction:

- Anger: What is the point of getting angry about small events? Be angry about larger issues—for example, the environment or inequality.

- Pride, ego: Take pride in being benevolent.

- Greed: Be greedy to serve.

- Cravings: Crave the truth.

- Aversion: Be averse to aversions.

- Jealousy: Let jealousy bring out the best in you.

- Intoxication: Get intoxicated with the Divine.

- Attachment: Let your attachment be to what inspires you.

Joy is love for what is.
Sorrow is love for what is not.

15. WHAT ENHANCES YOUR BEAUTY?

APRIL 30, 1997

BANGALORE ASHRAM, INDIA

When your mind isn't complaining, and instead is responsible, courageous, confident, and centered within, then you're inexplicably beautiful.

A person who can't act to correct an issue has no right to complain. And a person who can act to correct an issue will never complain.

Complaining is a sign of weakness.

Complaining is the nature of utter ignorance, that state in which you don't know the Higher Self.

Complaining takes away the beauty that's inborn in you. The negative effects of complaining show up more on the one who's on the spiritual path.

The worldly mind is a complaining mind; the Divine mind is a dancing mind. Just complaining without indicating the solution is irresponsible. And if the solutions aren't workable, finding alternative solutions is courage.

For external beauty, you put on things; for real Beauty, you have to drop all the things—including your complaints.

For external beauty, you put on makeup; for real Beauty, you only have to realize that you (and the world around you) are MADE UP!

NEWS FLASH:

Homes for the homeless and sanitation facilities for the village surrounding the ashram are the latest seva (service) projects initiated by Gurudev. Already fifteen houses are coming up fast.

A number of people asked Gurudev why he would sanction new houses for villagers when the ashram itself is already burdened with a need for more rooms. "The more rooms we have, the more people will come," he replied. "It is a never-ending shortage. If we say we will do seva only after our own needs are met, it will never happen." So, volunteers took on that project and made the whole village happy.

16. THE WAY OUT OF SORROW

MAY 28, 1997

MARSEILLES, FRANCE

If you're unhappy, check if one or all of these is lacking in you:

- Acceptance

- Centeredness

- Letting Go (of your small, individual needs and desires)

Acceptance is agreeing with the moment, total acceptance of all pleasant or unpleasant situations.

Centeredness means I want nothing, and I am nothing—I've dropped all the labels I put on myself.

Letting Go is "I am here for you, for your joy."

If you're grumbling, then these are lacking.

When you accept the situation, you can't grumble.

When you come from a state of centeredness (I don't want anything), you don't grumble.

And if you let go of your own needs, you'll have no complaints.

If you don't do these willingly, you'll do them later in desperation. First, you'll say, "Nothing can be done." Then next in anger, you'll say, "I give up; I want nothing," and finally, "I have no choice—to hell with it!"

> *All these three—acceptance, centeredness, and letting go—purify your mind and uplift you in joy.*

NEWS FLASH:

A full house in Paris sent a wave of enthusiasm all over France. Three cars and a bus departed for ten major cities on Gurudev's "Tour de France."

17. FEEL BLESSED

OCTOBER 23, 1997
HIGHWAY 7, BETWEEN BANGALORE
AND SHIMOGA, INDIA

Break through all the barriers and feel you're blessed. This is the one and only step you have to take—the rest will all happen.

This deep sense of feeling *I am blessed* can help you overcome all obstacles in life. You receive courage and confidence, and you open up for more blessings to pour in.

Once you realize you're blessed, then:

- All complaints disappear
- All grumbling disappears
- All insecurities disappear
- A sense of feeling unloved disappears
- Wanting love disappears

To make a difference in your life, feel you are blessed, especially for those on this path of knowledge.

This is the first step toward the Higher Self.

18. WHEN A MISTAKE IS NOT A MISTAKE

FEBRUARY 12, 1998
SINGAPORE

Blessed are those who don't see a mistake as a mistake!

When you make a mistake once, it's not a mistake—you've learned a valuable lesson. But when you keep repeating the same mistake over and over, it's a BIG mistake.

A mistake brings misery to you in the long run, so why would someone knowingly commit one? A "mistake" simply means you have "missed taking" a lesson that has come your way. Don't lament over it. Just take the lesson from it.

It's hard not to see your own mistakes. Outwardly you may justify yourself or plead innocence to someone else, but it pricks your conscience. Don't justify yourself. Instead, feel the prick of the mistake. That itself takes you out of the mistake.

When you point out a mistake to someone, do you see that person as separate from you and go on pointing out the error? Or do you make that person feel a part of you? Do your words add to their stress, or do they create more awareness in that person?

Often you don't point out a mistake when it's required—this is also a mistake. Pointing it out without consideration for the appropriate time and place is a mistake as well.

The fool keeps making the same mistakes again and again and never learns from them. Wise is the one who learns from one's own mistakes. Wisest is the one who learns from others' mistakes!

NEWS FLASH:

In Bali, Gurudev visited the ancient temple of Besaki, where, as in the old days, there is only the empty seat of the deity, signifying the Divine beyond form.

The Indonesian Director of Religious Affairs and a member of the Ministry of Education welcomed Gurudev at the opening of our Jakarta Ashram.

Art of Living volunteers from Jakarta have adopted an orphanage in Puncak. The director of the orphanage said that, while other people bring money, clothes, and toys, the Art of Living group supplied the missing nutrient that the children need the most: love! The children also received packages of school supplies and goodies. The group all laughed, sang, and danced as the director cried tears of gratitude.

Gurudev and the group traveling with him moved on to Singapore, where more than one thousand people welcomed him at the packed SLF Auditorium. The evening commenced with a traditional Chinese lion dance.

19. CONFUSION AND DECISION

APRIL 29, 1998

HAMBURG, GERMANY

A decision is required only when there's confusion. When there's no confusion, then there's no need for a decision.

If there's a piece of wood and a biscuit, you don't decide which one to eat, do you? Decision is always about choice, and choice is always confusing. The more decisions you have to make, the more confused you are, swinging between potential pain and pleasure.

> *In you, there is an actor, and there is also a witness to the actions.*
> *The actor is either confused or decisive, but the witness just observes*
> *and smiles.*

Action becomes spontaneous when the actor takes a back seat. The more the witness grows in you, the more playful and untouched you are. Then trust, faith, love, and joy all manifest in and around you.

Are you confused, decisive, or happy now?

20. GENEROSITY IS A QUALITY OF SPIRIT

JULY 1, 1998
VANCOUVER, CANADA

When you feel stuck in life and not growing, when you're bombarded by desires, when there's dryness, a lack of enthusiasm, no juice—what do you do?

Here's the solution: *Feel generous. Right away, not tomorrow.*

Generosity is a quality of the spirit. Both a prince and a pauper can feel generous. When you feel generous, your life becomes abundant, full of compassion and love.

Generosity and gratefulness are different. Gratefulness always has self-concern. You are grateful because you have something, or you get something.

Generosity is independent of external circumstances. No one else can make you feel generous—it is something you have to do yourself.

Generosity is not an act; it is a state of consciousness—but it always finds its expression in an act.

NEWS FLASH:

A successful Art of Living program for prison inmates is now in progress following Gurudev's visit to South Africa.

21. DON'T CORRECT YOUR MISTAKES—RECOGNIZE THEM!

OCTOBER 2, 1998

BANGALORE ASHRAM, INDIA

Often when we acknowledge a mistake, we try to justify it without taking responsibility for it. For example, we say, "To err is human," or "So what, everybody does it." Or we feel guilty about it and try to hide it.

Usually, in trying to correct mistakes, one gets caught up in more mistakes. Denial, justification, and guilt are the three traits that perpetuate a mistake.

Mistakes, when recognized, make one remorseful. Feeling the pinch and wanting to correct mistakes is good enough for one to be free from them. Those who recognize their mistakes are freed from them.

Recognize a mistake as an unconscious happening.

There may be mistakes or flaws in any action, situation, or person. Treat a flaw as you would treat a flower. Just as a flower has to wither away after some time, so does a flaw.

22. TRANSFORMING LUST

DECEMBER 3, 1999

COCHIN, INDIA

Lust is one of the main botherations that many people face. Lust grips the mind, tires the body, and dulls the intellect.

Lust, when indulged, brings inertia, and, when suppressed, brings anger. Lust is nothing but primordial unharnessed energy. The same energy, when harnessed, manifests as enthusiasm and sparkles as sharpness of intellect and love. Neither fighting nor encouraging lust, but instead sublimating it is a skill.

What are the factors that can transform lust into love?

1. Playfulness: People who are in the grip of lust can't be genuinely playful. When you are genuinely playful, there is no lust.

2. Generosity: When you realize that you are here only to give and feel generous, then lust is transformed. Lust makes one possessive and not generous.

3. Moderate to small intake of food.

4.   Remembrance of death.

5.   Divine love.

6.   Cold-water baths.

7.   Undertaking creative challenges.

23. WELCOMING AND RESISTING

JANUARY 21, 1999

EUROPEAN ASHRAM, BAD ANTOGAST, GERMANY

Do you welcome all that comes to you, or do you resist it?

You don't welcome all thoughts that come to your mind. When you welcome a thought, it means you find it good and will act on it. If you act on all the thoughts that come to your mind, you'll end up in a mental institution or prison. You resist or ignore some thoughts and welcome others. You need discrimination in life.

You can't resist everything, and you can't welcome everything. Welcoming and resisting are swings in life. Welcoming is essential for expansion and growth; resistance is essential for maintenance.

> *Audience member:* But what you resist persists!

> *Gurudev:* Not in the body. If you resist a cold, it doesn't persist. If there is no resistance in your body, you can't survive. Your body resists some things and welcomes others.

When the resistance is weak, the persistence happens. A strong resistance erases the opposition and leads to valor, power, and samadhi (equanimity). It brings in you the strength of a warrior. Nothing can tempt you; nothing can obstruct you. Where there is strong resistance or total welcome, victory is gained without any fight.

NEWS FLASH:

Today representatives of the Art of Living will be delivering a half-hour presentation at the United Nations World Health Committee in New York. Holland television has made a documentary on Gurudev.

24. THE NOISE OF NONVIOLENCE

APRIL 21, 1999

APPLE VALLEY, CALIFORNIA, UNITED STATES

Often violence comes with noise. Nonviolence happens in silence.

People who are violent make a lot of noise; they make it known. People who are nonviolent are quiet.

The time has come for people who are nonviolent to make noise so that violence will quiet down. The message of nonviolence has to come loud and clear so it can be heard from a young age.

A sense of shame has to be connected with anger and violence. The reason for anger and violence in young people is that it's associated with a sense of pride, not shame. They think it is prestigious or a status symbol to be aggressive.

This promotes aggression and violence, and as a result, human values are diminishing in society. Some movies and contemporary music glorify frustration, anger, and revenge and make these a role model for children.

We need to promote human values, especially love, compassion, and belongingness, loud and clear. Don't be shy or apologetic in talking about spiritual knowledge and practices as only spirituality can nurture human values.

> *Question*: If people are ashamed to be angry, won't that make them unnatural and bring a resistance to anger that will make it persist?
>
> *Gurudev*: If they're not ashamed, they'll feel they have a license to get angry and violent. Sometimes resistance is a good thing, like resistance to disease or resistance to bad habits.

NEWS FLASH:

Gurudev continued from Kauai to the island of Oahu, Hawaii, where meetings with government leaders awaited him.

The Hawaiian Art of Living prison program continues to flourish, and other new programs for government agencies are being planned.

Gurudev spoke at a luncheon honoring volunteer service leaders. He was interviewed on NBC-TV and was invited to speak at a youth conference with delegates from more than one hundred countries.

25. CHOICES AND CONFUSION

When you're in doubt, any activity you do will bring more doubts. When you have a choice, the grass on the other side will look greener, and this prevents you from enjoying what you have in your hand. When you're bothered by a choice, relax.

The choice is never between good and bad; it's always between bad and worse or good and better. Choices bring conflict, and there's freedom in "choicelessness."

How can you be centered when there is conflict? There's a Chinese saying: "When you're in doubt, take a pillow and go to bed!" Take a break, not just from activity, but also from the fruit (or result) of the activity. It will bring deep rest from doubts and conflicts.

26. TAKE IN AN ATOM

AUGUST 11, 1999
EUROPEAN ASHRAM, BAD ANTOGAST, GERMANY

The mind lives on "more." Misery starts with "wanting more and more." Misery makes you dense and keeps you on the surface level of life.

The Higher Self is subtle. To move from dense matter to the subtle, you go through the finest level of creation—the atom.

To overcome aversion, hatred, jealousy, cravings, or entanglements, you have to go to the atom, which means accepting a teeny tiny bit of all this creation.

It may be difficult to accept something you don't like, but you can definitely accept a tiny bit of it—an atom. This acceptance has to be done in a meditative state. The moment you accept that one atom, you'll see change happen.

This process can also help you feel more satisfied with those things you like in life. For example, suppose you love someone—you want more and more of them, yet there is no fulfillment. When you take in an atom, you're saying that just a glance, a word, or a moment will be good enough. When you're satisfied with that, it's enough to bring a shift, and there is fulfillment. Take just one atom of that person, and that's enough to bring fulfillment to you.

Though the river is vast, a little sip quenches your thirst. Though Earth has so much food, just a little bite satisfies your hunger. All that you need are tiny bits. Accept a tiny bit of everything in life—that will bring you fulfillment.

Tonight, go to bed feeling that you are satisfied, taking a tiny part of Divinity with you. Satisfaction comes from the subtle and not from "more and more."

27. WHO REACHES THE GOAL?

SEPTEMBER 1, 1999

BANGALORE ASHRAM, INDIA

Many people quit doing what they take on because they put their self-image, prestige, respect, comfort, and convenience ahead of their goal.

When do people give up?

- When they don't get the position they wanted
- When they get insulted
- When they feel they aren't getting what they expected
- When they consider working toward their goal a struggle rather than a challenge

And that's why only a few people in the world succeed in reaching their goal.

What's more important to you?

28. OVERCOMING DEPRESSION

NOVEMBER 26, 1999

INDORE, INDIA

Lack of idealism is the main cause of depression among youth today. Life appears to be so meaningless to these children, who are either too scared of the competitive world or too bogged down by heavy stimuli. They need inspiration, and spirituality is the inspiration that can keep the spirit up!

A fighting spirit is the antidote to depression. Depression sets in if there is a lack of zeal to fight.

Depression is the lack of energy; a fighting spirit and anger are bolts of energy.

If you're depressed, just fight for any cause.

If aggression crosses a certain limit, it leads you back into depression.

Wise are those who don't fall either into anger or depression. That is the golden rule of a *yogi*. Meditation keeps you out of both anger and depression.

Just wake up and acknowledge you are a *yogi*.

29. THE PROBLEM'S TAIL

FEBRUARY 3, 2000

OSLO, NORWAY

> *Gurudev*: There's no problem that can't be solved.
>
> *Audience member*: I have a few I can give you. (*Laughter*)
>
> *Gurudev*: When you have a problem and you think it can't be solved, you've accepted it—then it's no longer a problem; it's a fact.

For example, suppose you think it's a problem that the ocean in Norway is too cold. Obviously, you can't heat the ocean. If it can't be solved, you accept it, and it's no longer a problem.

The moment you realize there's no solution, a problem ceases to be a problem. That's why there's no problem that can't be solved.

The solution is the tail of every problem. Solutions come to you when:

- You're calm and collected

- You use intelligence

- You're active, not lethargic

- You have strong faith in the Divine plan

30. FEEL THE PINCH

FEBRUARY 17, 2000

BANGALORE ASHRAM, INDIA

Someone asked Gurudev, "Please forgive me if I've committed a mistake."

Gurudev answered, "Why should you be forgiven? You're asking for forgiveness because you feel a pinch, and you want to be free from it—is this not true? Let the pinch be there. The pinch will keep the mistake from happening again. Forgiveness removes the pinch, and you keep repeating the mistake!"

Question: How do you know a mistake is a mistake?

Gurudev: A mistake is something that gives you a pinch. If it hasn't pinched you, it's not a mistake at all. It's the pinch that irks the conscience, and that pinch disallows the mistake to be repeated. Be with the pinch and not the guilt. It's a very fine balance.

Question: What's the difference between guilt and a pinch?

Gurudev: Guilt is about a specific action, and a pinch is about what happened as a result of your action. You may feel guilty about what you did. You feel a pinch because of what happened either through you or even through someone else.

Question: How do we get over the guilt?

Gurudev: You can get over the guilt through wisdom, by knowing the nature of the mind, the nature of consciousness, and by having a broader perspective of the phenomenon.

Question: Can we learn from our mistakes without feeling the pinch?

Gurudev: Learning is at an intellectual level, while you feel the pinch at an emotional level. The drive of your emotions is much stronger than your intellect, so a pinch will not let the mistake recur.

Question: So, should we discard the intellect?

Gurudev: You cannot be driven by your emotions alone. Your intellect acts as a brake for your emotions.

Feel the pinch. The pinch will create awareness that what happened was beyond your capacity. The awareness will bring you to letting go, which will free you from guilt.

So, the steps of evolution are from pinch to awareness to letting go to freedom.

31. HOW TO DEAL WITH HUMILIATION

JUNE 27, 2000

MONTREAL ASHRAM, CANADA

When you have a sense of belonging, you don't feel humiliated. The more egotistic you are, the more humiliation you feel. When you're childlike and have a greater sense of kinship, you don't feel humiliated.

When you're committed to truth and not caught up in your ego, you also don't feel humiliated.

If you're afraid of humiliation, you can neither make progress in your material life nor in your spiritual life. Know that humiliation doesn't weaken you—it strengthens you.

Nobody can humiliate you unless you allow them to do so. When you stand above humiliation, you get closer to the self—to God. When you're steeped in love with existence, with the Divine, nothing whatsoever can humiliate you.

So, the way out of humiliation is:

- Don't resist it.
- Be childlike.
- Be silly.
- Get steeped in love with the Divine.
- Totally commit yourself to truth, to knowledge.

NEWS FLASH:

There was a silent retreat of 115 people and a teacher training course with seventy people at the Baikal Ashram in Siberia.

32. ARGUMENTS AND WRONG ACTION

JULY 12, 2000
LAKE TAHOE, CALIFORNIA, UNITED STATES

When a person is arguing, they shouldn't be given knowledge. An argumentative mind is not receptive to knowledge. When someone is in an argumentative mood, then giving knowledge or advice is in vain. In an argumentative mood, you feel you know it all. Then you're not ready for knowledge. That's why wise people don't give advice when they're in an argumentative environment.

Argument has a purpose. It can bring out the truth if there's no emotion or sense of "I" attached to it.

Argument can also have a disadvantage. It can make untruth appear to be truth.

The wise don't take arguments seriously; they simply have fun with them. Wisdom is beyond all arguments.

Both worldly and spiritual people will tell you not to do wrong, though the reasons they give are totally different.

A worldly person will tell you not to do wrong because it hurts him or others. A spiritual person will tell you not to do wrong because it would only harm you.

NEWS FLASH:

The mayor's office of the city of San Francisco gave Gurudev the highest commendation for his contributions to society and for the lasting impression he's left on the community of San Francisco and the world.

In satsang, a man asked Gurudev, "I do not feel the need for a guru (spiritual teacher). What is your opinion of people like me?"

Gurudev replied with a twinkle in his eye, "Don't take my advice!" (*Laughter*)

So, if he takes the advice, he has heeded the guru, and if he doesn't take the advice, then he's heeded him too. It's a paradox.

33. FALLING AWAY FROM AND COMING BACK TO THE SELF

DECEMBER 1, 2000

EUROPEAN ASHRAM, BAD ANTOGAST, GERMANY

When you're miserable, what's happened?

You've gone away from the Self. This is called *ashaucha*. It means you've become impure.

In India, when someone dies, the close relatives are said to be *ashaucha* for ten days because they're very sad. They're impure because they've moved away from the Self. It's believed that after ten days of grieving, reading the scriptures, and being with knowledge, they've purged out the impurities that came with those events. Pulling themselves back into the Self, they're now *shaucha*.

This happens again and again in life. You become *ashaucha*, and you have to get back to *shaucha*. Go deeper into yourself; then real *shaucha* happens.

Shaucha brings clarity of intellect, a pleasant mind, focused awareness, a say over the senses, and makes one eligible to realize the Self.

Shaucha is being disinterested in the habitual tendencies of your own senses. You have the understanding—*Oh yes, here's this old familiar tendency coming up again. Come on, I've had this experience enough, and still the body craves for it again.*

By being disinterested in one's own body and sense pleasures—just an idea, a sort of distaste—you'll find that the situation changes quickly.

Why do people love each other so much, have such an intimate relationship, and then fight? Because *ashaucha* has happened.

If you don't get a distaste for the tendency of the senses, then distaste for the object of the senses is bound to come; you'll blame the person or object.

Your attraction or craving to someone lasts only as long as you think that person is "other." When you think they're part of you, the attraction dies out. That's why in some couples, the husband or wife gets attracted to someone else because the partner has already become a part of them.

When you realize everyone is part of your Self, you enjoy the whole world without a sense of craving.

When *ashaucha* happens, come back to *shaucha* quickly. Whenever you get drowned in any worldly event, just remember: "I have become *ashaucha*; that's why I'm suffering in misery." Then come back to *shaucha*.

Your practices (meditation and SKY breathing), service, and *satsang* will all help you.

NEWS FLASH:

Gurudev was a major attraction, drawing large audiences at a science and spirituality conference in Basel, Switzerland.

Then, at the International Association for Human Values Conference (IAHV) in Amsterdam, Holland, Gurudev presented the Human Values Award 2000 to Max van der Stoel, the OSCE (Organisation for Security and Cooperation in Europe) high commissioner on national minorities. The IAHV conference was attended by several dignitaries, including the former prime minister of the Netherlands, who was one of the keynote speakers.

34. BACK TO SPACE

FEBRUARY 14, 2001
BANGALORE ASHRAM, INDIA

From time to time, the earth shakes and wakes us up from slumber—we who misuse nature and put our faith in bricks and mortar.

Your true security is in the Self, not in bricks and mortar. Earthquakes, floods, and volcanoes all drive home the truth that nothing is permanent and you can find no security in that which is impermanent. Disasters come to you as a shock and wake you up.

When such calamities occur, we try to understand their cause so that we can blame someone. Strangely, when you find someone to blame, you feel comfortable, but with natural calamities you can't blame anyone. They come to you as a shock. With wisdom, shocks can make you grow in leaps and bounds. Without wisdom, a shock can only lead you to negativity and depression.

Instead of questioning nature, wake up and see the opportunity for service. See what is happening in Gujarat now.[2] Today, hundreds and thousands are engaged in service activities that wouldn't have happened otherwise. One

---

2 A ninety-second 7.7 magnitude earthquake on January 26, 2001, killed thousands and displaced a million people in Gujarat.

positive thing coming out of destruction is the reconstruction of Gujarat, which wouldn't have happened if not for the earthquake. Another interesting outcome is a freshwater spring that appeared in a region that was continuously drought prone.

Wisdom is considering the earth as your beloved. Whether it shakes or breaks, it's dear to you. You always see good coming from it.

The four elements other than space—earth, water, air, and fire—create turbulence from time to time. If you depend on them for support, they'll shake you and lead you back to the space element.

Finding security in inner space is spirituality.

NEWS FLASH:

The Art of Living Foundation has adopted twenty-six villages in Kutch-Bhuj, the earthquake-hit area of Gujarat.

Research at the All India Institute of Medical Science showed significant changes in the brain wave patterns of the Art of Living teachers who participated in the study. All eighteen subjects were found to maintain high coherence and awareness during activity.

35. WHEN THINGS CHANGE

2009

BANGALORE, INDIA

Whatever is yours will always be yours. Anything that goes away was never yours to begin with. If you know this, you'll be at peace.

What is yours?

36. FROM ME TO WE

One thing that can be really helpful in coming out of depression is developing an attitude of service—thinking, *What can I do for society?*

Getting involved in a bigger cause shifts the whole focus of life and can take you out of the rut of "What about me?"

Happiness and success both depend on our ability to give.

37. CONSTRUCTIVE CRITICISM

Criticism should be from the throat, not from the heart. If it's constructive criticism, the recipient will take it in a good spirit.

If, from your heart, you wish for something bad to happen to someone, then you're only hurting yourself.

But that doesn't mean you should be superficially positive and never point out mistakes. If an apple is bad, it's insincere to say the apple is good. If someone asks you how the food was and you say it was very good even if you couldn't eat it, then that's not honest.

Where there is a problem, it must be pointed out, but without any hatred in your heart. Otherwise the feeling will only harm you.

The more you complain, the more energy you lose. Anything that's repeated sinks deeper into the consciousness. So don't let complaints go deep within.

38. OVERCOMING CHALLENGES

With the right approach and attitude, problems no longer remain problems, and solutions start presenting themselves. Problems are an inevitable part of life, and your ability to solve them with grace will always be a prized trait in all of the roles you play, especially those of leadership.

The wise have a different way of looking at problems. Remind yourself, "This too shall pass." This intelligence, to recognize the changing nature of the creation, is a sign of maturity.

Difficult times can bring out your hidden courage and potential in more ways than one. This valor will keep you afloat in the sea of changing and unchanging events. The feeling, "I have the power to handle it. Come what may, I will face it," is a powerful booster. When you summon this energy, self-doubt vanishes.

Realize that you are bigger than the problem. A problem appears too big only when you think you can't handle it. Look at those who have bigger problems; then yours will appear small.

Even after your valor has failed you, there's another way to move ahead—by offering or surrendering the problem to the Higher Power. Often we give up in frustration. Now try giving up in faith. Surrender is the realization that your effort can't bring forth all that you want in life. The big or great can't be had by the effort of the individual mind alone. Surrender brings a deep sense of ease, relief, and peace, and gives us immense strength to smile even through difficult times.

When the body, mind, and intellect are tired, you're unlikely to come up with a solution. That's why you need to pray, meditate, and move ahead with faith. Faith brings you stability, centeredness, calmness, and love.

Problems and challenges add charm to life and bring the best out of you. Learn from them and grow bigger than them.

39. THREE ASPECTS OF *KARMA*

JUNE 29, 1995
CALIFORNIA, UNITED STATES

Karma is an impression in one's consciousness. The impression draws similar situations, events, and actions to you. *Karma* has three aspects: action, impression, and result.

For example, you look at a banana. Looking at it is *karma* as an action.

You crave it and want to eat it because you've eaten it before. This is *karma* as an impression.

Then you eat it. This is *karma* as a result.

Looking at it, craving it, and eating it are all *karma*.

Unconscious action creates a chain of *karma*. Non-action can also create *karma*, but a conscious action transcends *karma*.

40. THREE TYPES OF *KARMA*

Question: Can we change our *karma*?

Gurudev: Some *karma* can be changed, and some can't.

When you make a cake batter, if there's too little sugar or butter, you can add more. If some other ingredient is too much, it can all be adjusted and repaired. But once it's cooked, it can't be reversed.

Milk can become yogurt—plain or sweetened—and plain yogurt can be sweetened. But neither can be reversed back to milk.

There are three types of *karma*:

> *Prarabdha is the action that is already occurring and is yielding its effect right now. You can't change it, as it's already happening.*
>
> *Sanchita is the gathered* karma *from the past. It exists as latent tendencies or impressions in the mind. Sanchita* karma *can be burned off by spiritual practices before it manifests.*
>
> *Agami* karma *is the future effect of the action. For example, if you commit a crime, you may not get caught today, but you'll live with the possibility that one day you may get caught.*

You are freed from *karma* when the impressions in the mind are erased.

> *Satsang, yoga, and meditation burn the seed of all negative* karmas *before they're given a chance to sprout.*
>
> *When you praise someone, you take on their good* karma. *When you blame someone, you take on their bad* karma.
>
> *Know this and surrender both good and bad* karma *to the Divine and be free.*

41. PAIN AND SUFFERING

Pain is inevitable; suffering is optional—you've heard that before, right? Pain is nothing but an intense sensation. Yet don't justify or encourage pain. Some people start justifying and encouraging pain, and that's where masochism starts. You need to stay clear of masochism, and that's why I say if pain comes, it's come due to some *karma*. That's it, move on.

The principle of *karma* is such a healthy thing to save the mind. It's such a good vaccination for the mind. When you say it happened because of *karma*, then you're able to let go and move on. Otherwise you brood over whatever has happened in the past.

42. SPONTANEITY AND FEVERISHNESS

Spontaneity is the sign of a vibrant life. When you're spontaneous, you don't chew on the past, you don't chew on yourself or others. If you get upset, it's okay, but it should be a spontaneous anger, not a stale one that goes on in your mind for months at a time, and then one day you burst! Anger should be like fire, fresh, not some stale thing you keep in your mind.

Children are like that; they're angry for a moment when you take a toy away from them—they're so angry, and then the next moment they're okay. Just stick to those tendencies that we came to this Earth with.

Relationships: Friends, Family, and the People in Your Life

1. LOVE IS NOT AN EMOTION

NOVEMBER 6, 1997

RISHIKESH, INDIA

If someone shows you a lot of love, what do you do?

1. You don't know how to respond.

2. You feel obliged and bound.

3. You shrink or shy away.

4. You feel foolish and awkward.

5. You try to reciprocate even though it's not genuine.

6. You doubt the love expressed or your worthiness.

7. You become afraid of losing respect because respect maintains a distance, and love doesn't allow distance.

8. Your ego hardens and doesn't allow you to receive and reciprocate.

9. You feel thrilled, and you want to have it all the time.

10. Anything else (fill in the blank).

The ability to receive love comes with the ability to give love. The more you're centered and know, through experience, that you are love, the more you'll feel at home with any amount of love that's expressed, in any manner.

Deep inside, you know:

Love is not an emotion!
Love is your very existence!

NEWS FLASH:

Art of Living course participants cleaned up tons of garbage from the banks of the Ganges River.

Indian teachers and organizers have resolved to start the following Sri Sri Seva Projects, and all satsang groups are invited to join:

1. Donate a minimum of 2 percent of personal income to charitable causes.

2. Contact supermarkets/stores and encourage them to discontinue using plastic bags.

2. RESPECTING OTHERS SHOWS YOUR OWN GREATNESS

FEBRUARY 18, 1998
BANGALORE, INDIA

When someone respects you, it's not because you possess some virtues; it's because of their greatness.

If you say God is great, it means YOU are great. God is already great—you saying so doesn't affect God.

When you respect someone, it shows your own greatness. To the extent you lack respect for people, your worth is that much less. If you respect everyone, your worth is that much more. Wise is the one who respects everyone.

Question: But, Gurudev, you can't respect a criminal!

Gurudev: Criminals should be respected too, as they teach you what not to do—at their own cost. Respect is a quality of refined consciousness.

3. SENSITIVITY AND STRENGTH

JUNE 18, 1997

MONTREAL ASHRAM, CANADA

Those who are sensitive often feel weak. Those who feel strong are often insensitive.

Some people are sensitive to themselves but insensitive to others. They often feel that others are the "bad guys."

Those who are sensitive to others but not to themselves often end up feeling helpless: "Poor me."

Some conclude it's better not to be sensitive because sensitivity brings pain—and they shut off. But be aware, if you're not sensitive, you'll lose all the finer things in life too—intuition, beauty, and the ecstasy of love.

Insensitive people usually don't recognize their weakness. And those who are sensitive don't recognize that sensitivity is their strength.

This path and this knowledge make you strong and sensitive.

Sensitivity is intuition.

Sensitivity is compassion.

Sensitivity is love.

Sensitivity is the real strength: calmness, endurance, silence, non-reactiveness, confidence, faith—and a smile.

Be both sensitive and strong.

NEWS FLASH:

From India: The children at the ashram school have the best test scores in the entire district, and the enrollment has doubled to 450.

4. KNOW YOUR TYPE

JULY 17, 2002

MONTREAL ASHRAM, CANADA

Normally people with similar tendencies group together; intelligent people group together, fools get together, happy people get together, ambitious people get together, and disgruntled people also group together! (*Laughter*) There's a saying, "Birds of a feather flock together."

The disgruntled people get together, complain, and pull one another down. A frustrated person can't be with those who are happy. You only feel comfortable when the other person is in tune with you. Intelligent people don't feel at home with foolish people. Foolish people feel that intelligent ones aren't sympathetic.

The wise feel at home with everyone—the disgruntled, the happy, the foolish, and the intelligent. Likewise, all types of people feel at home with the wise.

Just turn around and look at what goes on in your group of friends or your family—are you grateful or grumbling? Take responsibility to uplift the people around you.

The wise person is like the sky where all birds can fly.

5. THREE KINDS OF LOVE

APRIL 24, 1997
BANGALORE ASHRAM, INDIA

There are three kinds of love. That which comes out of charm, that which comes out of familiarity, and Divine love. Do you see what I'm saying?

Love that comes out of charm doesn't last long. The charm is born out of unfamiliarity or attraction, and once you become familiar, you quickly lose the attraction, and boredom sets in, like in many marriages. This type of love may diminish and bring fear, uncertainty, insecurity, and sadness.

Love that comes out of familiarity and comfort grows. You feel more comfortable, for example, with an old familiar friend rather than with a new person. But this love has no thrill, no enthusiasm, and no fire to it.

Divine love supersedes both of these. Divine love is ever new. The closer you come, the more charm and depth there is. Divine love has comfort, enthusiasm, and familiarity. There's never boredom, and it keeps everyone on their toes.

Worldly love can be like an ocean, yet an ocean has a bottom. Divine love is like the sky—limitless and infinite. From the bottom of the ocean, soar into the vast sky.

6. DON'T MAKE A MISTAKE BY POINTING OUT MISTAKES

AUGUST 29, 2000

NEW YORK, UNITED STATES

Don't tell a person a mistake he knows that he made. What's the use of pointing out a mistake that he knows he has committed? By doing this, you'll make that person feel more guilty, defensive, or resentful, and this will create more distance.

You should only point out the mistake of a person who doesn't know but wants to know. Also, don't point out the mistake of a person who knows but doesn't want you to know about it. Often people know the mistakes they've committed, but they don't want you to tell them.

Before pointing out a person's mistake, think about the usefulness of your comments. See whether they'll in any way help to improve the situation, foster love, or bring harmony.

A magnanimous person doesn't pick on the mistakes of others and make them feel guilty. Instead, they correct others' mistakes with compassion and care, not through words but through their attitude.

NEWS FLASH:

Washington, D.C., had big satsangs and a lovely boat ride with Gurudev.

The D.C. mayor's office and Senator Paul Strauss presented an honor to Gurudev at the elegant ballroom of the Capitol Hilton in the presence of 1,500 people.

At the United Nations in New York City, Gurudev was given a standing ovation after his talk, in which he spoke about how spirituality was the fruit of the banana and religion was the peel. Later, people were asking each other, "Are you the banana, or are you the peel?" One person was heard commenting, "I am the monkey; I get both the banana and the peel!"

7. MISTAKES

JULY 12, 2001
LAKE TAHOE, CALIFORNIA, UNITED STATES

Mistakes keep happening all the time. Often you get irritated by them and want to correct them. How much can you correct? There are two situations when you correct others' mistakes:

1. You correct someone's mistake because it bothers you. But even if you correct it, this doesn't work.

2. You correct someone's mistake, not because it bothers you, but for their sake so that they can grow.

To correct mistakes, you need authority and love. Authority and love seem to be contradictory, but in reality, they're not. Authority without love is stifling and doesn't work. Love without authority is shallow. A friend needs to have both authority and love, but they need to be in the right combination. This can happen if you're totally dispassionate and centered.

When you allow room for mistakes, you can be both authoritative and sweet. That's how the Divine is, the right balance of both. Krishna, Jesus, and all the enlightened masters have both. People in love also exercise authority with those they love. Authority and love exist in all relationships.

8. DEALING WITH BLAME

AUGUST 10, 1995
BRAUNLAGE, GERMANY

How do you feel when someone blames you? Hurt, unhappy, sad, heavy? And when someone blames you, what do you usually do? You blame them back, or you put up a resistance in yourself.

Yet whatever you resist, persists. You may not show an outward reaction, but you may be resisting inside. It's fine to resist outside but don't resist from within—you'll immediately feel lighter.

When someone is blaming you, it could be because of ignorance, erroneous perception, or envy. There is an ancient belief that when someone blames you, they take away your bad *karma*.

If you understand this, you won't worry about being blamed. If you resist when someone blames you, you're not allowing them to take away the negative *karma*.

Don't repeat the negative stories that someone tells you about someone else. Don't believe in them. Discourage them. And if someone blames you directly, don't believe what they say. Just know they're taking away your bad *karma* and let it go.

When you blame someone, you take on their bad *karma*. When you praise someone, you take on their good *karma*. Surrender both good and bad *karma* to the Divine and be free!

The ignorant person says, "Don't blame me" because it hurts him. An enlightened person also says, "Don't blame me." Do you know why? Because it might hurt you.

NEWS FLASH:

Gurudev arrived in Poland for a beautiful silent retreat with nearly four hundred people. Many people were moved to tears with gratitude. After that, Gurudev came to Braunlage, Germany, where more than two hundred people are now celebrating silence.

9. HOW TO DEAL WITH RUDE BEHAVIOR

DECEMBER 5, 1996

THIRUVANANTHAPURAM, KERALA, INDIA

What do you do when someone behaves very rudely toward you?

- Get upset
- Act rudely back
- Get frustrated
- Run away and avoid the person or situation
- Blame the person

- Preach to the person

None of these will strengthen you in any way. So, what are the options? See rude behavior in this light:

- It indicates their passion, the intensity of their commitment.

- It indicates their stress and insensitivity.

- It projects the upbringing of the person.

- It shows a behavioral pattern they're stuck in.

- It shows lack of awareness, of knowledge.

- It shows a lack of observation of the mind and its sensations.

- It shows you the behavior to avoid.

- It is an opportunity for you to resist the reactive tendency and strengthen your mind.

- It can be a test for your equanimity.

- It is an exercise for you to welcome and absorb the rudeness.

- It strengthens your mind.

- It reveals the love that you are as unconditional.

The next time someone is rude to you, give them a big smile. If you can digest their rudeness, nothing whatsoever can shake you.

10. FRIENDSHIP FOR A REASON

MAY 23, 2002

JAKARTA, JAVA, INDONESIA

Examine your friendships; they're often made for a reason. For example:

- You make friends because you have common enemies. Fear or a threat to survival can bring people together.

- You make friends because you have common problems. You talk about your problems and become friends. For example, sickness or job dissatisfaction, etc.

- People get together and become friends because they have common interests, for example, through business or a profession (doctors, architects, social workers, etc.).

- You make friends because of common tastes. You have similar interests in sports, movies, music, entertainment, hobbies, etc.

- People become friends because of compassion and service. Out of compassion and pity for someone, you become friends with them.

- People become friends merely because of a long-term acquaintance.

Brave are those who nurture friendships for only friendship's sake. Such friendships will neither die nor become soured, for they're born out of one's friendly nature. Only through wisdom can one uncover one's friendly nature.

11. JUDGMENTS AND GOOD COMPANY

JUNE 26, 1996

MONTREAL ASHRAM, CANADA

Though you've heard "don't judge," judgment happens unavoidably in day-to-day life. You either approve or disapprove of people's actions and behavior.

But always remember that everything is changing, and don't hold on to the judgment. Otherwise, your judgment gets solidified like a rock. It brings misery for you and for others.

If judgments are lighter, like a breeze, they bring in fragrance and then move away. Or they could bring a foul smell, then move away. But they shouldn't stay forever.

Judgments are so subtle that you're not even aware of their existence. Judging or labeling someone as judgmental is also a judgment. Only in the state of Being, in a state of expanded consciousness, when you're full of love and compassion, can you ever be free from all judgments.

Yet the world cannot move without judgments. Until you judge something as good or bad, you can't take any action. If you see rotten apples in the store, you say they're no good and you only buy the good ones. If someone lies to you ten times, you think that the next time he speaks it could also be a lie. Judgment happens automatically.

See the possibility that people and things can change at any time, and don't hold on to judgments.

You need to judge your company. Your company can lift you up or pull you down.

The company that drags you down toward doubt, dejection, blame, complaints, anger, delusion, and desires is bad company.

The company that lifts you up toward joy, enthusiasm, service, love, trust, and knowledge is good company.

When someone complains, first you listen, then you nod, then you sympathize, and then you also complain.

Your company can create hell for you in heaven or heaven for you in hell. You be the judge.

12. DEVELOP THE EYES THAT SEE BEAUTY

AUGUST 24, 1995
LONDON, UNITED KINGDOM

There is a certain mindset that always finds faults. Even with the ideal companion or the most beautiful painting, such a person will find something wrong. This kind of mindset is called *asuya*; it can never know the sacred spiritual knowledge.

Asuya is finding fault or seeing a malicious intent everywhere. Suppose it's windy and you shut the door, but at that moment someone else was just about to walk in. He'll think that the door has been slammed in his face! This is *asuya*.

Even after ten years of friendship, you find some fault and decide to break it off. Now you don't see any good from that entire relationship. This is *asuya*.

The moment you're out of the spiritual path, you feel that everything on the path was all wrong. This is *asuya*.

Asuya is when a child says, "Mother, you don't love me!" The child's vision is wrong; if the mother doesn't love the child, who will? It frustrates the mother.

Knowledge is different at different levels of consciousness. At a particular point, you become *anasuya*.

Anasuya means being devoid of fault-finding eyes.

From a distance, it's easy to miss a fault in somebody; up close, no fault escapes you. Even craters can't be seen from afar; up close, even a smooth surface has imperfections. If you're only interested in the holes, you won't see the magnitude of things.

If you aren't in *anasuya*, knowledge can't blossom in you. Then there's no point in giving knowledge.

If a mirror is dusty, you can clean it. But if your eyes have a cataract, no amount of dusting the mirror will help. You have to remove the cataract. Then you'll see that the mirror was already clean.

Asuya—fault-finding eyes—gives you the idea that "the whole world is not sharp; the whole world is no good."

Anasuya is knowing that "it's my own vision of the world that's blurred." And once you discover you have the wrong vision, half of the problem has already disappeared.

13. A LIAR IS INNOCENT

SEPTEMBER 6, 1995
BANGALORE ASHRAM, INDIA

A dear person you trust lies to you, and you catch him. What do you feel?

- Sadness
- Anger
- Cheated
- Disappointment
- Compassion
- Let down
- Loss of respect
- Wonder
- Shock
- Embarrassment

Yet when someone is caught lying, he's not a good liar. Had he been a good liar, he wouldn't have been caught. He is so innocent that he couldn't even lie properly. He lied and got caught! If he hadn't been caught, how would you ever know he was a liar?

So . . . you can never know a good liar. The person you call a liar is not a good liar and is innocent. Isn't he?

You needn't go through all the previously-listed mental gymnastics. Instead, melt and dissolve in love.

14. RESPECT VERSUS FREEDOM

JULY 30, 1997
GERMAN ACADEMY, BAD ANTOGAST, GERMANY

> *Question*: What do you do if people don't respect you?
>
> *Gurudev*: Thank them. They have given you freedom. (*Surprised laughter*)

When people respect you, they often take away your freedom. They expect you to smile at them, recognize them, and behave in a certain way with them.

When people don't respect you, you're not obliged to answer their questions, and you can drop all formalities. You can naturally smile or frown—you can just be.

When people love and respect you, you're obliged to return their courtesies because you don't want to hurt them. When they don't respect or love you, they won't be hurt by your expressions. They set you free.

You often gain respect at the cost of your freedom. Wisdom is to put freedom first and not bother about respect.

> *Question*: Won't freedom bring arrogance?
>
> *Gurudev*: True freedom isn't an "I don't care" attitude; it's not stiff. It's an inner lightness with a genuine smile. When someone is stiff and arrogant, they're not free. Love blossoms only in freedom.

When there is love, respect simply follows you.

15. CONFLICT AND INNOCENCE

AUGUST 18, 2000
BANGALORE ASHRAM, INDIA

Fights can only happen among equals. When you fight with someone, you make that person your equal. But in reality, there's no one like you. When you keep people either above or below you, then there's no fight.

When people are above you, you respect them. When they're below you, you love them, and you feel compassionate.

Either submission or compassion can take you out of a fight in no time. This is one way to look at a situation when you're tired of fighting. But when you're rested again, see it as a game, and just fight and have fun!

The same is true of the mind. When the mind is caught up in the senses or thinks it's equal to the senses, there's constant conflict. But when the mind is smaller than the senses, as in animals, there's no conflict. And when it realizes that it's bigger than the senses, there's no conflict. When the mind transcends the senses, it comes back to its true nature, which is innocence—"in no sense."

Does this make sense? (*Laughter*)

NEWS FLASH:

Malawi, in central Africa, became the newest country to join the Art of Living family. The Discovery Channel filmed in the Bangalore ashram.

16. SINGING, COMMUNICATION, AND EGO

AUGUST 19, 1998
GEILO, NORWAY

There are three modes of communication: In head-to-head communication you talk, in heart-to-heart communication you sing, and soul-to-soul communication happens in silence.

When you meet with people, you often keep talking and blabbering— keeping the communication at the head level.

But when you're out in nature, you start humming or singing, and your communication comes through the heart.

And when you're with a spiritual teacher, you go blank and forget all the questions, and communication happens through the soul in silence.

When you meet with people, you tend to remain in the head. Many don't feel comfortable singing with others (except when it's organized, like a chorus)—your ego obstructs you. Yet, when you do sing with people, you move to the heart or feeling level.

Some feel comfortable just listening to music; many sing only when they're alone. A few people sing to attract attention or to charm.

All this comes from ego. The Sanskrit word *bhajan* ("devotional song") literally means sharing—authentic sharing from the deepest level of our existence. If you sing with people, your ego shatters. Children can do so because they don't have an ego. To sing with a stranger, you have to be free of ego.

Head level is safe for the ego; heart level breaks the ego; soul level dissolves the ego. All communication failures happen because of ego.

> *Exercise: When you're with people, rather than chatting, just start singing and feel the shift of energy that happens. If you want to have more fun, greet a stranger with a song.*

NEWS FLASH:

The Art of Living hosted a United Nations roundtable in Geneva on the Art of Making Peace. An Art of Living prison program is starting in Denmark. Several research scientists came and met Gurudev.

17. TRUE LOVE EXPECTS NOTHING

True love is always one-sided. True love is not expecting anything in return from the other person.

If you want something in return from the other person, it becomes a barter system. Doing something to get something is business. You give, then demand. Demands destroy love. In demanding love, you are destroying it.

18. HOW TO CONQUER JEALOUSY OR ENVY

AUGUST 4, 1999

EUROPEAN ASHRAM, BAD ANTOGAST, GERMANY

There are many ways to conquer jealousy or envy:

1. Know that the person you're jealous or envious of has done some good *karma* (action) in the past and is now reaping the fruit.

2. See it as an inspiration to gain merit yourself.

3. Feel a sense of belonging with them. See that they are a part of you.

4. Think of all you have that they don't have and feel grateful.

5. Close your eyes and take a few minutes to observe the sensations associated with jealousy that you feel in your body.

6. Join hands and form a team with them.

7. Realize that, in the current of moving time, all will perish.

8. Think of everyone who is jealous of what you have and see if what they envy has really brought you any great joy.

9. Go and ask them, "Are you happy?"

Question: And what if they say, "Yes"?

Gurudev: If the answer is "yes," then they must be on a spiritual path! (*Laughter*)

Question: What should we do if others are jealous or envious of us?

Gurudev:

1. Praise them in superlatives.

2. Create a sense of belonging in them by your kind actions.

3. Know that all feelings and emotions are just passing clouds.

4. It's best not to recognize their envy or jealousy at all. If you recognize a feeling as a reality, it only magnifies it and makes your ignorance grow.

5. Don't show off your talents to them.

6. Know that they're puppets. They'll all perish like apples and tomatoes—just with a longer shelf life.

If nothing else works, take a pillow and go to bed . . .

19. SAVE YOUR MIND AT ALL COSTS

I want to ask you a question. Many times, you say something, but you don't mean it, right? What if people hold on to your words and don't see beyond your words? Would you like that? You wouldn't. You want them to see beyond your words. Do you do that? Not much. You hold on to their words. You don't like others to hold on to your words. You want them to see beyond that. But you hold on to others' words.

You don't give them the benefit of the doubt. What they're saying, they may not be really meaning it. We've spoiled many friendships like that, haven't we? Hasn't this taken a big toll on your friendships? Because we hold on to what they say, we don't see what's beyond that. Those who are just connected with someone's words aren't good friends. They're very superficial.

This is the sign of a civilized, cultured person, that you don't just lock on to someone's words and harp on them. When you were growing up, your mother, at her wit's end, may have said, "Get lost!" But if you really got lost, imagine her state! She'd have a heart attack. Don't give too much importance to words. Learn to see beyond the words.

People are hungry in their emotions. They're hungry for recognition. They're hungry for things they don't even know they're hungry for, and so they say and do things that they don't even mean. Why don't you give them a little space? Accommodate them. It's okay. Then you'll save your mind.

This is our mantra: Save your mind at all costs! If you save your mind, you can win over any situation. So, give the benefit of the doubt to people. If they say something, don't lock on to their words and hold on to them and hold it against them. It's okay. You've made mistakes. Let them make some mistakes. Never mind!

20. JUST ASSUME PEOPLE LOVE YOU

Don't question others' love for you. Don't ask for proof. Take it for granted that the other person loves you. Demand destroys love.

If you feel that your partner or spouse doesn't love you as much as before or their attention has reduced, don't ask, "Do you really love me? You don't love me these days like you did in the old days." You know, it's such a big load for someone to prove their love for others. If someone asks you to prove your love, you'll say, "Oh my God! How do I prove that to this person?"

Instead, see and acknowledge how much they love you. Even if the love has dried up inside them, it will be rekindled. They'll see your magnanimity, your understanding, and will start loving you more. Do everything with some style and a smile.

Often love is thought to be between two people—you and the other person. When there's another, it means you don't feel totally one with the person. You always question and doubt the other person's love for you. If you doubt whether the other person really loves you or not, you'll be unable to love them unconditionally, unable to merge with them.

Certain things you have to take for granted. One thing is the love of the other person from whom you want love. You have to take it for granted. Even if the love is not there, you must feel that it is there.

Divine love means feeling totally one with the other. Be indifferent to anything that appears to be opposing it.

21. HOW TO MAINTAIN INTIMACY

NOVEMBER 29, 1995
BANGALORE ASHRAM, INDIA

What breaks intimacy?

1. Ego (pride) or taking a position
2. Obsession with your own desire
3. Taking intimacy for granted
4. Finding imperfection in oneself or others
5. Expectations
6. Insensitivity or oversensitivity
7. Lack of discretion or centeredness
8. Judgments
9. Grumbling or lack of gratitude

How can you maintain intimacy?

Intimacy brings a no-mindedness in you: The mind dissolves, and you experience the vastness. It brings you to the moment. Don't gripe about the events and hold the other person responsible. Go beyond the events.

Look beyond the events, meditate, and be in the moment. Be magnanimous. Don't complain—instead engage in creative activities, appreciate others, make it a habit to uplift their enthusiasm, and make room to accommodate flaws. When you love someone, you take it for granted that they love you.

This is the way to maintain intimacy.

22. A FRIEND IS A FOE, A FOE IS A FRIEND

MARCH 19, 1997

RISHIKESH, INDIA

To do their best, a policeman, a judge, and a king can't have friends. In the company of your friends, you lose your centeredness. It's your enemy that puts you back into your Self.

Your friend sympathizes with you and makes you believe in matter. Your adversary makes you feel helpless and takes you to the spirit. So, your foe is your friend, and your friend is your foe!

NEWS FLASH:

In Urugalli, Karnataka, doctors in the Art of Living community conducted a free medical camp; 2,500 villagers were diagnosed and given medicines.

23. WITH WHOM ARE YOU AT EASE?

JULY 9, 1997

MONTREAL ASHRAM, CANADA

With whom do you feel really comfortable and at ease?

With someone who does not question your love, someone who takes for granted that you love them. Isn't it?

When someone doubts your love, and you constantly have to prove it, this becomes a heavy load on your head. They start questioning you and demand explanations for all your actions. To explain everything you do is a burden. Your nature is to shed the burden because you don't feel comfortable.

When you question the reason behind someone's action, you're asking for justice for yourself. You create a distance when you ask for justice. Your whole intention is to come close, but instead, you create a distance.

That's why it's futile to demand an explanation or give an explanation.

If somebody is just there with you, like a part of you, they don't question you—they're like your arm. There is a closeness and unity that goes beyond all demands and questions.

24. WHEN YOUR LOVE HITS A WALL

NOVEMBER 13, 1997

JAIPUR, INDIA

When you feel a lot of love for somebody, and they don't accept it, what do you do?

- Get frustrated

- Turn the love into hatred and wish for revenge

- Again and again, remind them how much you love them and how little they love you

- Become fussy and cranky

- Throw tantrums

- Feel humiliated, and try to save face

- Resolve never to love again

- Feel hurt and mistreated

- Try to be aloof and indifferent

And you'll have seen that none of these work! They only make it worse. What is the way out of this? How can you maintain your lovingness?

- Have patience.

- Be centered and limit your expression of love. Sometimes an over-expression of love puts people off.

- Change your expression of love.

- Take it for granted that they love you and accept their style of expression. Like a mother of three children—one child talks, one child doesn't talk, and one child throws tantrums—her love for each child is constant regardless of their behavior.

- Genuinely acknowledge their love for you—this will turn your demand into gratefulness. The more grateful you are in life, the more love comes your way.

- Know that hurt is part of love and take responsibility for it.

- Realize that when you move away from your center you'll feel miserable.

25. WHY DO YOU RESPECT SOMEONE?

FEBRUARY 29, 1996

BANGALORE ASHRAM, INDIA

Why do you respect someone?

Because of their good qualities, right? Like honesty, wisdom, love, talent, behavior. But all these change in time. And when they change, you lose respect. You often only respect greatness.

I have tremendous respect for each and every person. Not for their greatness or wisdom or talent, but for their very person. I respect everyone totally. So I can never lose respect for anybody, however they may be.

One doesn't need to be great in order to be respected. Respecting life itself makes you great.

Don't look for respect from others; that makes you weak.

Have respect for your Self, and no one can take away your self-respect.

NEWS FLASH:

On to Copenhagen, the capital of Denmark. It was a media event; people from TV, radio, and the newspaper filed into the hotel, and the TV crew followed the Art of Living group to packed and lively public talks.

From Stockholm, Sweden: A TV crew came into the meditation hall to interview Gurudev. They asked him what he thought about the New Age and if Art of Living was part of the New Age. With a mischievous smile, Gurudev replied, "Age is always new."

One of Sweden's most respected TV journalists for a major channel featured Gurudev and the Dalai Lama. Evening talks bubbled with humor, brilliant questions, and laughter.

26. THE LOVE OF THE IGNORANT, THE ANGER OF THE ENLIGHTENED

AUGUST 31, 1995
HERE AND NOW

The love of the ignorant can be harmful, yet even the anger of the enlightened is not harmful—it can only be good!

An example from the free school at the Art of Living Center in Bangalore, India: 250 children are enrolled, but only two hundred come to class on any given day. Fifty children don't show up. Why? They cry at home, "Mother, I don't want to go to school."

The mother gives in, saying, "Oh, la la, don't cry . . . okay." She thinks, *No child in the world is like my child.* She gives in to the immature demands of the child and defends him. She doesn't see the long-term value of discipline and education.

So, what happens? The child grows up spoiled and will never learn the alphabet and to read or write. And the mother says, "Oh, never mind, there are sheep to look after and fields to tend." The love of the ignorant can cause more harm than good.

On the other hand, the anger of the enlightened is a blessing.

The *Puranas* (ancient symbolic stories) give many instances of this. There was once a Master traveling with a disciple in the middle province of India. During their travels, some rude, rough, and abusive boys began throwing stones and teasing the disciple, calling him names. This went on for some time as the boys followed the Master and the disciple.

They came to a river. The Master and the disciple got into a boat and started to cross. The boys got into another boat that began to sink in the middle of the river.

The Master slapped the disciple across the face. The disciple was so sur-prised, as he hadn't said a single word in response to the boys' taunts! He'd been such a good disciple, and yet the Master had slapped him.

The Master said, "It's your fault. You're responsible for their boat sinking. You didn't respond to their abuse. Nature has now punished them in a worse way because you didn't have enough compassion to quell their insults."

That slap from the Master took away the *karma* of this event so that it would not be carried into the boys' future. It also served to take away any little bit of joy the disciple may have felt as he was seeing the boys' boat sink! Thus, it also took away the *karma* of the event for the disciple. When you don't react but consciously respond with compassion, you take away *karma*.

So even the anger of the enlightened is a blessing!

27. LOYALTY

AUGUST 4, 1998
EUROPEAN ASHRAM, BAD ANTOGAST, GERMANY

Loyalty is a quality of a mature and integrated mind. Loyalty indicates undi-vided consciousness and shows a richness of the mind. A divided mind lacks wholeness, which is essential to health, and can gradually lead to mental and physical disorders.

When the mind isn't integrated, it's feverish, disloyal, and opportunistic.

Disloyalty comes out of opportunism—being shortsighted about one's destiny.

Loyalty brings strength and will give you the support of Nature in the long run.

Fear and ambitions are impediments to loyalty.

Loyalty is needed both on the material and spiritual planes—it's essential to create, maintain, or transform any institution, group, or society.

Loyalty means believing in the continuity of commitment. It takes you beyond the duality of craving and aversion.

Responsibility, dedication, and commitment are its limbs.

28. WHY DO YOU LOVE SOMEONE?

AUGUST 12, 1998

EUROPEAN ASHRAM, BAD ANTOGAST, GERMANY

Do you love someone because they're great or unique? If so, I tell you, you're hopeless! (*Laughter*)

Why do you love someone? Is it because of their qualities, or is it because of a sense of kinship or intimacy?

You can love someone for their qualities and not feel a sense of kinship. This type of love gives rise to competition and jealousy.

If you love someone for their qualities, that love is not stable. When the qualities change or when you get used to the qualities, love gets shaky, and it also changes. Loving someone because of their greatness or uniqueness is third-rate love.

However, if you love someone out of kinship—because they belong to you—then that love remains for lifetimes. Loving someone because they belong to you, great or otherwise, is unconditional love.

People say, "I love God because He is great." This isn't a big thing. If God is found to be ordinary, just one of us, would your love for God collapse?

If you love God because He's yours, then however God is, whether He creates or destroys, you still love Him. The love of kinship is like the love for yourself.

> *Question*: Many people don't love themselves, so . . . ?
>
> *Gurudev*: No! It is the other way around. They love themselves so much that they want better qualities and a better appearance for themselves. This love of qualities makes them hard on themselves.

Spiritual knowledge and practices, service, and satsang bring about a sense of belonging in no time. When love springs forth from a sense of belonging, then the actions and qualities do not overshadow love.

Neither qualities nor action can be perfect all the time. Love and a feeling of kinship alone can be perfect.

NEWS FLASH:

An Art of Living course will be offered at Nova University in Florida as part of their regular curriculum.

29. WHAT ARE THE SIGNS OF LOVE?

NOVEMBER 5, 1998

NEW DELHI, INDIA

When you love someone, you don't see anything wrong in them. Even if you see some fault in them, you justify the fault and say, "Well, everyone does it! It's normal." You think you haven't done enough for them. The more you do, the more you want to do for them. They're always in your mind.

Ordinary things become extraordinary, for example, a baby winking at its grandmother. You want them to be yours exclusively. When you love someone, you want to see them happy always, and you want them to have the best.

30. LOVE'S WISDOM

FEBRUARY 12, 1999

BANGALORE ASHRAM, INDIA

"I chant the name of my beloved in every breath. The beloved is faultless—perfect."

—MIRABAI, *sixteenth-century Indian poet*

When there is so much love, you take total responsibility for any misunderstanding. You may express dismay for a moment on the surface, but when you don't feel that in your heart, you arrive at a perfect understanding. You're in a state where all problems and differences slide away, and only love shines through.

Usually, we get stuck in our differences because we've lost sight of ourselves. In the name of love, we try to manipulate and control the other person. It's natural that when we love somebody, we want them to be perfect.

You never see the holes in the ground from the top of a hill; from an airplane, the earth looks so smooth. Likewise, from a state of elevated consciousness, you don't see the flaws in others. But if you come to the ground, you easily see the holes. And to fill the holes, you have to see them. You can't build a home being airborne. You can't till the land without looking at the holes, filling them, and removing the pebbles.

That's why when you love somebody and are close to them, you find faults in them. But instead of helping them to correct themselves, we tend to run away.

When you love somebody and see their faults, stay with them and help them—this is wisdom.

31. LOVE AND LUST

MARCH 4, 1999

RISHIKESH, INDIA

In love, even an object gains life. Stones speak to you; trees speak to you; the sun, the moon, and the whole creation become alive.

Any obsession devoid of love, including sex, is lust. In lust, even a living being becomes a mere object. You even want to use people like objects.

Love and lust are so close, yet so different! Lust brings tension; love brings relaxation.

Lust focuses on the part; love focuses on the whole.

Lust brings violence; love brings sacrifice.

In lust, you want to grab and possess; in love, you want to give and surrender.

Lust says, "I want you to do what I want." Love says, "I want you to do what you want."

In lust, there's effort; love is effortless.

Lust causes feverishness and frustration; love brings longing and pain.

Lust imprisons and destroys; love liberates and sets you free.

Lust demands; love commands.

Lust gets you mixed-up and confused; in love, you are focused and spaced-out!

Lust is dark and monotonous; love has many modes and colors.

If someone's lust is interrupted, they get angry and start hating. Hatred in the world today isn't out of love—it's out of lust.

Love is playfulness, and in lust, there is cunning and manipulation.

During the ancient *Holi* festival in India, everybody celebrates by throwing colored powders and water on each other, realizing that life is full of colors. We play many roles in our lives; if all the roles get mixed up, it becomes dark, like when you mix all the colors. The wise play each role distinctly, just as colors displayed side by side form a rainbow.

32. LOVE AND RENUNCIATION

JUNE 30, 1999

MONTREAL ASHRAM, CANADA

Only one who has renounced can truly love. The degree you've renounced is the degree to which you have the ability to love.

Often people think those who renounce can't love, and those who love can't renounce; this is because so-called renunciants don't seem to be in love, and so-called lovers are very possessive and seem to be in need.

True love is non-possessive and brings freedom. Renunciation is nothing but freedom, and only in freedom can love fully blossom.

When in love, you say, "I only want this and nothing else." Renunciation is, "I want nothing."

In love there is no other need. Renunciation is having no need.

Love and renunciation, although appearing to be opposites, are two sides of the same coin.

> *Question*: Does this mean the lover renounces his beloved?
>
> *Gurudev*: You renounce the attachment, the possessiveness. Renunciation doesn't diminish love; it enhances it. Only renunciation can sustain love and joy. Without it, love turns into misery, possessiveness, jealousy, and anger.

In renunciation, you become centered and content; contentment sustains love. Without renunciation, one gets discontented, frustrated, sad, fearful, suspicious, and analytical. And the whole soap opera begins. And this is what we find in society, don't we?

The so-called renunciants have run away from life frustrated and disappointed. Real renunciation is born out of wisdom—i.e., seeing life in the larger context of time and space.

NEWS FLASH:

In the aftermath of the Kosovo War, two Art of Living teachers planned to go to Belgrade and Kosovo.

33. THE VALUE OF SAYING YOU'RE SORRY
DECEMBER 28, 2000
EUROPEAN ASHRAM, BAD ANTOGAST, GERMANY

Often, in wanting to be right, you're insensitive to others' feelings. When someone's hurt, arguing with them and trying to prove that you're right will be in vain. By simply saying "sorry," you can uplift the other person and take away the bitterness. In many situations saying "sorry" is better than trying to prove you're right—it can avert much unpleasantness.

This one word of five letters, when said sincerely, can remove anger, guilt, hatred, and distance.

34. REVERENCE AND OWNERSHIP
SEPTEMBER 20, 2001
BANGALORE ASHRAM, INDIA

Often you don't have reverence for that which you are close to or familiar with. Even if you've had reverence, you seem to lose it over a period of time.

Whatever you revere becomes bigger than you. When you have reverence in all your relationships, your own consciousness expands. Then even small things appear to be significant. Every little creature appears to be dignified. It's the reverence in every relationship that saves the relationship.

When you have reverence for the whole universe, you're in harmony with the whole universe. Then you don't need to reject anything.

When you have reverence, you complain less.

Reverence in closeness and familiarity frees you from greed, jealousy, and lust. Cultivate the skill of having reverence every moment in your life.

NEWS FLASH:

In Simla, nestled in the foothills of the Himalayas, Gurudev was received by a moving traditional welcome with horns, music, and dances. There he gave an address to senior government officials at the State Guest House. In Lucknow, wheelchairs and hearing aids were given to five hundred physically challenged people.

35. LOVE AND TRUTH

FEBRUARY 22, 2001
BANGALORE ASHRAM, INDIA

Why does someone lie to their close ones or their beloved?

This is a question often asked by lovers. Love can't stand untruth, causing relationships to break up when this happens. The answer lies in understanding the paradox of love and truth.

A lady came to me and said that her husband lied to her. She was very upset.

I asked, "Why does your husband lie to you? He lies to you because he loves you and is afraid to lose your love or hurt you. If he didn't love you, he wouldn't lie to you."

People tell lies to save and maintain their love. The fear that the truth might damage their love causes lies to be told between husband and wife, boyfriend and girlfriend, parents and children, and in other family situations.

In love you feel weak, but truth brings strength. Yet why do people prefer love over truth—weakness over strength? (*Laughter*)

No one wants to sacrifice love. So people are ready to give up the truth for their love. Love takes the luster out of truth. Sometimes the truth can make love bitter, while in love even lies can appear sweet.

The truth that doesn't nourish love makes no sense, and the love that can't withstand the truth is not true love.

When one is assured that their love is so strong that the truth can neither break it nor cause bitterness, then truth prevails and love shines.

With truth there are judgments, but love is beyond judgments. Thus, true love makes you weak, and yet it is the greatest strength!

NEWS FLASH:

The beautiful South Indian state of Kerala saw overflowing stadiums, inspiring talks, and deep meditations at Gurudev's satsangs. All the events were highlighted in the media. The chief minister of Kerala State and most of his cabinet ministers hosted Gurudev at a special function and sought his advice on problems they were facing.

In an outdoor venue in Thiruvananthapuram, when the participants opened their eyes after practicing SKY Breath Meditation, they could not see Gurudev on the stage, though they could hear his voice. Later, they found him, seated on the lower branch of a tree with a cordless microphone!

36. UNREQUITED LOVE

One-sided love is considered unfortunate. I say, lucky are those whose love is one-sided. The love that withstands rejection, without turning into bitterness, is real love. It liberates you. But with such love in your heart, you no longer look for liberation.

37. FIND DEPTH IN SILENCE

The experience of love, or true gratitude, can't be expressed in words. Real beauty, true friendship has no words. Have you ever sat, just in silence, with somebody whom you love? Do you remember having driven silently with somebody in the car, just looking at the beauty, the sunset, the hills, the ocean?

Instead, we open our mouths, start chatting, and destroy all the beauty that's there. When you drive, see how many conversations go on in the car. There are four people, and there may be two conversations going on. Sometimes all four people are talking.

Your presence speaks of your essence and what you are. A great philosopher may give discourses on love, but you wouldn't feel that. If you're just there, being in love, it spreads to everyone.

Sit within yourself, meditate, keep some silence, and experience that you *are* love. You're made up of a substance called love. Transcend the words, then love appears. Be simple, innocent, and all gets done through that power of love.

We can communicate in silence very well. We can communicate through our hearts very well. With the silence inside, you can hear the birds and the rhythm of their song. A bird sings in rhythm without any drums or beat. It's so perfect and melodious.

Go a little deeper, and there's music going on within your own body. Divine music is happening in our own bodies, but we're not aware of it.

There is so much beauty we're missing in our lives if we haven't lived in that sphere of silence within us. Every day, set everything aside for ten minutes and just look at the sky; look at the stars; look at the roses.

Don't say, "This rose is beautiful, this one is big, and that rose is bigger." It's *there*; that is it. It's beautiful. There's so much to life . . . the day we realize words are insufficient, we've gone deeper into existence and gained some depth in life.

38. RESPECT AND INTIMACY IN RELATIONSHIPS

If you observe your experiences, you'll see that your emotions are ten times stronger than your intellect, than your thinking. You may decide, *Okay, I won't do this; I'll commit*. But when the time comes, your emotions are so powerful. They come like a tornado and just wash away all that you had thought about in the past.

Marriage is not something you decide up here (*Gurudev points at his head*). It's not a job of your upper chamber. It's somewhere deep inside. Isn't it? You feel attracted. You fall in love with someone. And then you decide to be together.

Now, when you're together, what really happens? You have to examine this situation. Somehow in your being together more and more, the attraction dies out.

Love manifests in three forms. First is attraction. And then on the mental level, a little higher is love, the emotional attachment. And then the spiritual dimension of it is devotion or selfless love, the final dimension. Culmination of love from attraction to devotion.

Now what happens when you are attracted? You're together so much that your attraction dies out. And love somehow seems to have disappeared.

Not only love disappears, but also respect. You respect something that is a little away from you, but as you come together, you don't seem to respect the person so much.

Love brings intimacy, but in the intimacy, respect is lost. Yet every individual is striving to have respect in life. This is the main problem in marriage. You may still have love, but you have a difficulty in maintaining your respect or you feel you have been less respected.

So one has to understand love. One has to *live* love. Understanding means not intellectually understanding, but being aware of all the dimensions; then life blooms. It takes a different turn.

Without that, marriage will definitely not be what it promises to be or do what you think it will do for you: take out the loneliness, make you fuller, make life more supportive and enriching. It won't do that . . .

39. COMPASSION

When someone hurts you, you hate them. But why did they hurt you? Because they're hurting. They have lots of wounds and hurts inside, and all they can do is hurt others.

Why do criminals commit crimes? Because they're in pain, because they need healing, because they're not normal, because they're sick. They have no understanding or clear perception of themselves.

When you see what's going on inside them, your hatred will fall off. You'll only have compassion.

If you see somebody agitated or angry, have you ever felt compassion for them? No one ever likes feeling agitated or angry. Feeling that way is not pleasant for them.

If we don't feel compassion when we see others' mistakes, we're bound to get angry ourselves. The cause of anger is the lack of total knowledge of what's happening inside that person.

Showing anger itself isn't wrong, but being caught up in anger only hurts you. There's a difference. Sometimes you can show anger purposefully. With your children, you can act tough or maybe shout at them if they put themselves in danger. There's a place for showing anger, but when you actually become angry, what's happening to you? You're shaken completely.

Are you ever happy with the decisions you've made or the words you've spoken when you're angry? No, because you lose your total awareness. If you're completely aware and you are acting angry, that's fine.

The type of anger that turns into fear and hatred comes when we don't know the situation totally, when we don't put ourselves into the other person's shoes.

I'm not saying these emotions are good or bad, right or wrong. We're just looking at what the consequences are.

Acting in the World:
How to Handle Life's Events
and Situations

1. REST AND ACTIVITY

SEPTEMBER 10, 1998

BANGALORE ASHRAM, INDIA

Activity and rest are two vital aspects of life; balancing them is a skill in itself. Knowing when to have what and how much to have, is wisdom. Finding them in each other—activity in rest and rest in activity—is the ultimate freedom.

The memory of hard work is more tiring than the work itself. Thinking you've worked hard interferes with the quality of rest.

Some people take pride in just working hard, without any achievement. And there are others who crave a long rest, not knowing that true rest is in non-doership (not getting caught up in your personal role in the actions you take or in the outcome). It's the *quality* of rest, even if it's short, that recuperates you.

When rest is needed, your body will automatically take it. Resting without thinking about the need for it is more restful.

> *Question*: Our work is very stressful. We don't get enough time for the family. What should we do?
>
> *Gurudev*: Do you spend quality time with your family? Even if you spend half an hour, are you cordial and fully attentive to the needs of our family? It is not the length of time you spend with your family that matters. It is the quality that matters.

Thinking you need rest makes you restless.
Thinking you have to work hard makes you tired.
Thinking you have worked hard brings self-pity.

Contentment, centeredness, and the experience of the Self are the deepest rest.

2. SIMPLE OR COMPLEX?

MARCH 26, 1997

RISHIKESH, INDIA

Life is utterly simple and yet most complex. You have to simultaneously attend to both facets. When life appears most complex, turn to simplicity; simplicity brings peace. When you're peaceful, attend to the complexity; that will make you more skillful.

If you're only with simplicity, it makes you lazy and dull; growth isn't there.

Being only with complexity makes you angry and frustrated; there's no life at all.

The intelligent ones skillfully balance these two and rejoice in both.

When you recognize both the simplicity and the complexity of life, you'll be skillfully peaceful!

White light is pure simplicity.
The colors of the prism are the complexity of life.
When your heart is pure, your life becomes so colorful.

3. WHAT MAKES A REAL VACATION?

MARCH 31, 2002

NEW DELHI, INDIA

Rest and happiness make a real vacation. Often people go on vacation and return tired and tanned, needing a few more days to recuperate. A true vacation energizes you and doesn't wear you out.

Remember, nothing energizes you like wisdom.

• Doubts and complaints are impediments to rest.

- The moment you set out on your vacation, know that it has begun. Often people expect to find a pinnacle of happiness. Enjoy every moment of the journey as children do; don't wait for the destination.

- If you can't be happy in one place, you can't be happy in any other place. If you don't know how to row one boat, you won't be able to row any other boat.

- To get the most satisfaction out of your vacation, you need to do something creative and engage in *seva* (service).

- Don't ever forget to make meditation and gratitude to the Divine a part of your vacation. If your days are holy, then every day is a holiday!

NEWS FLASH:

In Delhi, Gurudev addressed the Progress, Harmony, and Development (PHD) Chamber of Commerce and Industry and several top Muslim leaders. Later, Gurudev visited the tomb of the famous Sufi saint Khwaja Nizamuddin Auliya and was accorded a reception at the Fatehpuri Masjid (a seventeenth-century mosque).

4. WORDS

APRIL 18, 1996
BALI CLIFF RESORT, BALI, INDONESIA

We attach meaning to words and distort them.

For example, the word *disillusioned*. It's good when you become disillusioned. You're out of the illusion and have come to reality. The meanings of words change over time. The word *enthused* came from ancient Greek, meaning "God is within us." Then *enthused* came to mean "crazy," and today the meaning of the word has changed again.

Don't be stuck with words. Your worries are words; your ideas are words. Wisdom is beyond words. It's your very Being, the essence of all that's expressed in words. See and relate beyond words—then truth dawns in your life!

If you manipulate words, it's a lie;
If you play on words, it's a joke;

If you rely on words, it's ignorance;
If you transcend words, it's wisdom.

NEWS FLASH:

In Bali, Gurudev received a royal welcome at the venue with traditional dance and garlands. Press and TV crews came to the hotel and splashed the news throughout Indonesia. Gurudev invited the media to join the silent retreat, and they came out with big smiles. Now some are organizing Art of Living courses.

The silence generated from the retreat was so profound that hotel employees themselves spontaneously started observing silence, communicating with retreat participants only through gestures and notes.

5. WAKE UP AND SLOW DOWN

APRIL 7, 2002

GANGTOK, SIKKIM, INDIA

Often you're in a rush in life. When you're in a rush, you're unable to perceive things properly—this takes away the charm, thrill, and beauty from your life. You can never be close to the truth when you're in a rush because your perception, observation, and expression become distorted.

The rush to enjoy robs the joy from life. It denies the happiness and freedom of here and now. Often you don't even know why you're in a hurry. It almost becomes a biological phenomenon to be in a rush. Wake up and become aware of the rush in you!

It's ridiculous to be in a rush to slow down. Just being aware of the rush itself will take care of it. Slowing down doesn't mean procrastination or lethargy, though it's easy to be at the extremes of either rushing or lethargy.

The rush in you is due to feverishness, and feverishness arises out of lack, a need to achieve, whereas dynamism is an expression of fulfillment.

The golden rule is to be awake. Being awake you can't help but be dynamic.

NEWS FLASH:

On the way to a satsang in Itanagar, Gurudev visited the local Nyishi, tribal people who pray to the sun god.

6. TOLERANCE AND ACCEPTANCE ARE NOT VIRTUES

JANUARY 21, 1998

WILLIAMS ISLAND, FLORIDA, UNITED STATES

Many people think tolerance is a virtue.

Tolerance is a negative term. Tolerance indicates a deep sense of dislike. If you like something, there is no question about whether you tolerate it.

When you're tolerating something, it means you're temporarily putting up with it. Tolerance is a potential volcano; you're just waiting to explode.

At any time, tolerance can turn into hatred. Tolerance indicates a sense of separateness, small-mindedness, and limited awareness.

Acceptance can also be seen as negative. You accept only that which is not lovable.

> *Question*: Don't you need a sense of self-assurance to love people?
>
> *Gurudev*: Only the Self is always assuring. Nothing else! This is our company—the Self-Assurance Company!
>
> *Question*: Aren't we supposed to accept people as they are?
>
> *Gurudev*: If you don't love them, you will have to accept them. The words *tolerance* and *acceptance* are considered positive; I say they are not. Tolerance and acceptance come with judgment and separation.

Don't accept people as they are or tolerate them. Just love them as they are! If you can't love them, at least accept them and be at peace.

NEWS FLASH:

From Suriname, Gurudev moved on to Bogota, the capital of Columbia. After an interview for national television, the host of the show said that she has to change her whole series, which was entitled *Tolerance*.

7. THE EIGHT WEALTHS

DECEMBER 21, 1995

GYANMANDIR, BANGALORE, INDIA

There are eight types of wealth:

1. Wealth as *material comfort*: Some inherit this type of wealth, while some have to work for it.

2. Wealth as *health*: Some people have money but keep falling sick. In this situation, material wealth is immaterial. Some may not have much money but have enough to eat and are healthy.

3. Wealth as *success*: Some may be born into a very wealthy family, but they face failure in whatever they do. Success is another form of wealth.

4. Wealth as *courage*: See life as an adventurous game and play without worrying about the outcome. If you're afraid of making mistakes and therefore don't act, you lack the wealth of courage. There'll be no fun in life even if there is a lot of money.

5. Wealth as *friendliness*: Having a caring attitude and a sense of belonging is a great blessing. One may have other types of wealth but will still feel lonely and fearful if there is no sense of belonging.

6. Wealth as *skill*: Effort alone is not enough. You need the wealth of skill. People may do all they can yet fail to achieve their goals. Skillful people know how to manage their mind, people, and situations.

7. Wealth as *dignity*: The world is full of lessons if only we observe it with full awareness. Be humble; then nothing can touch you. No one can humiliate you. In the eyes of the Divine, it is those who serve creation that are the true kings and queens. Walk like a king and be a perfect servant!

8. Wealth as *memory of the source*: We're unaware of our source. We only know that we were born; we don't know how we were born. Our memory is very short—we forget the eternal nature of life. The moment we become aware of our source and our own infinite nature, our whole life transforms. It's like someone suddenly realizing how wealthy he is.

8. AN AWKWARD SITUATION

MARCH 4, 2002

NEW DELHI, INDIA

Why do you feel awkward? How do you get out of it?

You may feel out of place if you've always been the center of attention and are suddenly sidelined.

Similarly, you may feel uncomfortable if you've always been on the sidelines and are suddenly pushed to center stage.

You may feel awkward if you're accustomed to ordering others and suddenly have to take orders, or if you usually follow orders and then are made to give them.

A very busy person with nothing to do or a laid-back person who is faced with responsibilities may experience unease. Very often feeling out of place blocks reason and distorts logic.

If the situation you're in is inevitable, tolerate it.

If it's avoidable, walk away from it.

If you feel that it can expand your abilities, smile through it.

Every awkward situation pushes you beyond your boundaries and is a test of how deeply you're established in wisdom.

Willingly going through an awkward situation will increase your comfort zone. No one will be able to push your buttons, and you'll become centered and unshakable.

NEWS FLASH:

Gurudev visited the village of Massaudi, which has been the target of numerous insurgent attacks. Thousands there have benefited from Art of Living's workshops. Villagers shared that it was impossible to leave their homes after dusk because of the volatile, dangerous situation, but that the workshops and community gatherings had transformed their lives.

Following the Gujarat tragedy, Gurudev requested that everyone observe two minutes of silence at a specific time throughout the world for communal peace and harmony and to pay respect to those who were victims of religious intolerance.

9. THE SUBTLE TRUTH ABOUT VIRTUES

FEBRUARY 8, 2001

BANGALORE ASHRAM, INDIA

If you observe your behavior, you'll notice that you procrastinate when doing something good but hurry when it comes to doing something bad. For example, if you're angry, you want to express it immediately.

Do you know why? Because virtues are your very nature, and they'll never leave you. But your vices aren't your nature, and they will leave you. Negative tendencies are transient and will leave you if you don't act on them. Frustration and crying can't stay long, especially with the same intensity. Perhaps you're concerned that your vices will leave you if you don't act on them!

It is wise to postpone acting on vices, for they won't stay, and to act immediately when doing good; otherwise you'll continue to postpone doing good—maybe for the next few lifetimes. (*Laughter*)

NEWS FLASH:

There was an attempt during the World Economic Forum to divide the religious communities into monotheistic and polytheistic. This was given up at Gurudev's insistence, and harmony finally prevailed.

10. POLITICS

JANUARY 14, 1998

PARAMARIBO, SURINAME

Wherever there are people, politics is inevitable. Don't let politics sway you away from the spiritual path. If you're afraid of politics, you can't be successful in the spiritual realm. You have to cross the barricade of politics. It's the test of your strength, commitment, and your focus. You can't avoid politics, but it's your choice whether to harbor it in your mind or not.

There was politics among the twelve apostles and with Buddha. Krishna was in politics from head to toe. You say you don't want politics? The more you don't want politics, the more you'll harbor it in your consciousness.

When you recognize politics in any group, that's a blessing for you to be centered and go inward. You can do that without blaming the group and running away from people or chickening out. It can enhance your skill to act and not get attached.

ADVANTAGES OF POLITICS:

- Brings up diversity in people
- Puts in front of you different viewpoints, ways, and tendencies
- Enhances your skill to communicate and act
- Brings centeredness and dispassion
- Shakes you up and makes you apply spiritual insights and wisdom
- Enhances your capacity to accept and tolerate
- Makes you realize that this whole life is a game

The strong will smile through the politics, and the weak will lament. Cross the threshold of politics and come to the Self.

NEWS FLASH:

In Trinidad, the prime minister and two other cabinet ministers met with Gurudev, expressing their gratitude for our work, and offering their wholehearted support.

Then, in Croatia, Gurudev addressed the interreligious conference organized by the parliamentarians of the country, followed by satsang at the beautiful Sheraton Hotel, filled to capacity. Gurudev met with many dignitaries, and TV people from Croatia filmed a documentary.

11. IS LIFE SHORT OR ETERNAL?

APRIL 28, 1999

SANTA BARBARA, CALIFORNIA, UNITED STATES

The realization that life is very short brings dynamism into your life. Unwanted things fall away, as well as distractions and procrastination. When you have to act or use effort, know that life is short.

The ignorant person does it the other way; he hurries for the result and is impatient and frustrated. Anytime you're in a hurry, you can't enjoy life. Impatience goes away when you know that life is eternal.

WAKE UP! LIFE IS TOO SHORT!

Time is running out, so what are you doing with your life? Is your life useful to you and the world around you? Realize life is too short.

WAKE UP! LIFE IS ETERNAL!

When you're looking for results, know that time is eternal.

When you're looking for a return of a favor or a result from your good deed, you want it quickly. But when you know that there are many years in your life— and even many lifetimes—you realize that you'll get it sooner or later.

When it comes to hope, you should know that there are many lifetimes. If someone doesn't thank you or takes advantage of you, thank them because they'll pay you back later with interest. So no one needs to feel sorry that they have been taken advantage of or unappreciated. Know they will have to pay you back in the future.

When it comes to enjoying the fruit of your actions, good deeds, or even blessings, know that life is eternal.

NEWS FLASH:

In addition to the jubilant satsangs in Apple Valley, Los Angeles, Santa Barbara, Monterey, Berkeley, and San Jose, Gurudev spoke on human values in the twentieth century at the University of California in Santa Barbara. A new initiative has begun to promote the Art of Living course for youth in high schools and colleges throughout the USA.

12. ACTION AND REACTION

JULY 27, 2000
EUROPEAN ASHRAM, BAD ANTOGAST, GERMANY

Action comes out of conscious decision. Reaction comes out of impulsiveness. Impulsiveness creates a chain of *karma*.

Reaction and non-action both create *karma*, but conscious action transcends *karma*.

Although conscious action doesn't create new *karma*, non-action can. For example, a soldier at war and a policeman using tear gas don't create *karma*; they're doing their *dharma* (fulfilling their duties). But a doctor who doesn't give medicine to a patient in need incurs *karma*.

Through knowledge and devotion, transcend all *karma* and be free.

13. "IMPORTANT" AND "UNIMPORTANT"

JANUARY 11, 2001

MONTREAL ASHRAM, CANADA

Too many people are stuck with what is "important." Why do you always have to do only that which is important?

For something to be important, there need to be many things that are unimportant. You can't eliminate unimportant things. It's important to have unimportant things to make something else important. (*Laughter*)

Things are either themselves important, or they make other things important. So that means everything is important, and nothing is important.

When you say something is important, you limit your vastness.

A journalist asked me, "Why is it important to breathe? Why is it important to be happy? Why is it important to have peace?"

These questions aren't relevant at all. Why should you always look for what's important? Something unimportant can contribute to something that is important. And what's important and unimportant changes with time and space. Food is important when you're hungry and unimportant when you're full.

When something is inevitable, you don't categorize it as important or unimportant. It's beyond choice.

"Everything is important" is the path of service. "Nothing is important" is deep meditation.

NEWS FLASH:

Two African countries, Benin and Togo, have entered the Art of Living family, bringing the total number of countries to 112.

A person in the Montreal Art of Living group who is a cab driver by profession picked up a passenger one night who appeared overcome by drugs and
alcohol. The passenger demanded to be taken to his destination for half-fare,
and when the driver protested, the passenger pulled a gun.

At first the driver was afraid, but when he looked at the photo of Gurudev
on the dashboard, he felt completely protected. During the drive, the passenger
put the gun away. Eventually, he asked who the person in the photo was. When
they reached the destination, the passenger bowed his head in respect toward
the picture and paid the full fare to the driver along with a handsome tip.

14. FREE WILL AND DESTINY

JULY 3, 2002
WASHINGTON, D.C., UNITED STATES

When people consider the past as free will, they're filled with remorse and
regret.

When they consider the future as destiny, lethargy and inertia set in.

A wise person will consider the past as destiny, and the future as free will.

When you consider the past as destiny, no more questions are raised, and
the mind is at ease. And when you consider the future as free will, you're filled
with enthusiasm and dynamism.

Of course, there will be some uncertainty and anxiety when you consider
the future as free will. But it can also bring alertness and creativity.

Consider the past as destiny, the future as free will, and the present
moment as Divinity.

> *Question*: How do we remove the anxiety?
>
> *Gurudev*: By having faith in the Divine and doing your spir-
> itual practices.

NEWS FLASH:

The Art of Living played a leading role in the World Sustainable Development
Summit 2002 held in Johannesburg, South Africa. The team was greatly
appreciated.

More than one hundred Art of Living volunteers from seven European countries came together to help flood victims in Dresden, Germany, where huge floods have destroyed all that people once had. Many volunteers worked through the night to free houses from the mud. The mayor of Pirna/Dresden and the leading military officer there have expressed their gratitude to the Art of Living volunteers.

Currently, free Art of Living trauma relief courses (for youth and adults) are being conducted for the flood victims.

15. INTENTION, ATTENTION, AND MANIFESTATION

Whatever you put attention on will start manifesting in your life. Intention, attention, manifestation—that's how the universe works.

Our life runs through intention. Everything we do has a desire, an intention, or an unconscious habit attached to it. Whether you want to drink a glass of water, take a walk, or watch TV, first an intention arises in the mind.

Make an intention and leave it to the universe. If you go to temples or where there's a fountain, they say, "Make a wish and drop it." You drop the coin in the fountain.

In the same way, an intention has to be dropped. Have an intention and consciously drop it. It will start manifesting. If you hold on to the intention, it becomes desire, and desire brings feverishness and heartache.

Intention, attention, and manifestation go together. Wherever you put your attention, that will grow. Feeling you have abundance, abundance will grow. When you put your attention on lack, lack will grow. If our attention is consistently clinging to negativity, that's what's going to grow.

If your attention is always on the negative, switch it to the positive. Just being aware of it, it already switches. Then give the time for it to manifest. Meditation is the skill in which you learn how to drop the intention and relax.

16. BEING OPEN-MINDED

Question: During business negotiations and workplace interactions, how does one say no with a "yes-mind"?

Gurudev: To be in yes-mind doesn't mean agreeing to anything and everything. Being in yes-mind means being very open and positive, listening, and not being closed-minded. You lend your ears to what others have to say and what others are saying. That is part of a yes-mind. But yes-mind doesn't mean that you agree to things that people say that don't make sense. You hear what they say, but if it doesn't make sense, you say no. That's still a yes-mind.

17. ORGANIZATION

DECEMBER 17, 1998

BANGALORE ASHRAM, INDIA

The entire creation is a huge organization. Everything is made up of atoms. The whole world is nothing but organization in which the atoms have decided to organize themselves in a specific pattern to form a particular substance. And those particular patterns bring them specific qualities.

Death, decay, and transformation happen when the atoms get bored with patterns and decide to reorganize themselves. For example, when the atoms of the apple say, "Enough of being an apple," that's when the rotting starts. If there's no boredom with patterns, there can be no decay.

The movement from one organized state to another is also organized— this is the transient organization that we call chaos, and it may need a catalyst. Spiritual knowledge is such a catalyst. So, you have absolutely no escape from organization.

18. FIVE PLACES TO VISIT BEFORE YOU DIE

Every human being should spend five days of their life in these five places:

1. **A Farm:** Spend one day morning to evening with a farmer. See what he does all day. Just be in the dirt, sowing seeds, and watching how seeds sprout. You need to have patience to see a seed sprout. One day may not be enough. Doing this will make you sensitive toward the environment and toward food.

2. **A Jail:** Everyone should spend one day in jail with those who have been convicted of crime. Be with them. Talk with them. It'll become evident that inside every culprit, there's a victim crying

for help. Compassion will arise in your heart. Your life will be transformed. They have nobody to come sit with them, talk with them, heal their wounds, and transform them. One day in prison will open your vision—your prejudice will go, and your tendency to condemn people will disappear.

3. **A School:** Spend one day in a school or with children who have special needs and try to teach them something. They'll make many mistakes. You need a lot of patience to be with young children. Wherever you are in life, there are so many that you can help and guide. This brings deep satisfaction.

It's not only those with long hair and beards who can be gurus, or teachers. Everybody can play the role, at least for someone. You don't really need specialized skills, but you need compassion. Being a teacher, you can channel that compassion. "I want nothing but that my student should progress." Such unconditional love comes to your life.

4. **A Hospice or a Cemetery:** Spend one day with hospice patients, at a cemetery or a funeral home. You'll have a very close and intense experience of life's impermanence. Whatever complaints you carry around will vanish. Having the knowledge that death can come anytime will change your perspective for good.

5. **A Mental Institution:** Spend one day in a mental institution and see what all the patients say. Would you take what people there say seriously? Whatever anybody in a mental hospital says to you, whatever names they call you, you won't take that to heart.

Most of our troubles are because we take people's words too seriously, either what they say or don't say. After spending a day when anybody can say anything to you, you'll develop greater strength to face criticism without being shaken. Not only will you be strong enough to accept all criticism; you'll also have compassion for those who criticize you.

You should have the courage to give criticism and receive criticism as well. If we teach our children this, they'll grow into strong and stable members of society.

19. THE OTHER SIDE OF FEAR

MARCH 1, 2001

UDAIPUR, JAGMANDIR, INDIA

Nature has inbuilt some amount of fear in all living beings. This fear makes life defend and protect itself. Like salt in food, a little bit of fear is essential for people to be righteous.

> *Fear of hurting someone makes you more conscious.*
> *Fear of failure makes you keener and more dynamic.*
> *Fear moves you from carelessness to taking care.*
> *Fear moves you from insensitivity to sensitivity.*
> *Fear moves you from dullness to alertness.*

A total lack of fear may lead to destructive tendencies. Someone with a distorted ego knows no fear, and neither does someone with expanded consciousness.

There's a difference, like that of heaven and earth, between these two fearless states. When you're in love and have trust in the universe, there's no fear. The ego dismisses fear and moves in a destructive manner. The wise one acknowledges fear and takes refuge in the Divine.

Fear makes you righteous; fear keeps you on the path; fear keeps you from being destructive. Peace and order are maintained on the planet because of fear.

A newborn knows no fear; it totally relies on its mother. When a baby starts becoming independent—whether it's a child, kitten, or bird—it experiences fear and goes running back to the mother. This is inbuilt by nature to sustain life.

So, the purpose of fear is to bring you back to your source!

NEWS FLASH:

In Ahmedabad, Gurudev's meeting with the chief minister and bureaucrats proved extremely useful. Gurudev suggested drastic changes in the layout plan of the nine hundred quake-hit villages that are to be rebuilt. His ideas were greatly appreciated and immediately incorporated.

20. IGNORANCE OF YOUR CAPABILITIES CAN EXPAND YOU

OCTOBER 18, 2000

BANGALORE ASHRAM, INDIA

Always know that the Divine never gives you a responsibility that you can't fulfill. No one ever expects you to treat them if you're not a doctor. No one will ask you to fix their wiring system if you're not an electrician.

Your responsibility is only what you can do. And you don't know what you can do. Always accept that you don't know all that you can do.

Ignorance of your capability can expand you.

When you know what you can do, you can progress. But when you don't limit yourself to what you think you can do, you can grow by leaps and bounds.

When you know what you can do, you can do things. When you don't know what you can do, you can do things even better!

21. LOVE AND AUTHORITY

AUGUST 16, 2001

BANGALORE ASHRAM, INDIA

Love and authority are totally opposite values, yet they coexist.

The less refined the consciousness, the more pronounced the authority must be. The more refined and subtle the consciousness, the less need there is to exercise authority.

When you're unrefined, you demand that others give you authority, and when you demand authority, love recedes. Asserting authority indicates a lack of confidence and love. The more evident one's authority, the less sensitive and effective it will be.

A sensible person will not demand authority at all but will assume it. The most effective CEOs won't make you feel their authority, for authority can never bring inspiration.

Your sincere servant has more authority over you than your boss, isn't that so? Just like a baby has full authority over his mother.

The subtler your consciousness becomes, the more authority you gain. The greater the love, the subtler the authority will be. The lesser the love, the more pronounced the authority will be.

NEWS FLASH:

This week 2,400 prison inmates in Tihar Prison, the largest prison complex in South Asia, are taking the Art of Living course. This is the largest Art of Living course to date, requiring twenty teachers.

Recent research conducted by Dr. H. Geetha, professor of biochemistry at the Bangalore Medical College, shows a marked improvement in cholesterol levels after practicing SKY Breath Meditation.

22. PRAISE THE FOOLS

MARCH 22, 2002
RISHIKESH, INDIA

Praising the fool is beneficial to society!

A fool, when pleased, might stop doing harm and start doing good work. In this sense, it's wise to praise fools as they need motivation. Your praise is meaningful when it's directed toward a fool.

The wise, by their very nature, will continue doing good work because their attitude doesn't depend on someone's praise or blame. It serves no purpose to praise a wise person because your praise will have no impact on him.

There are three types of people—the wise, the crooked, and the immature.

The wise continue doing good work, whether scolded or praised. The crooked ones need to be praised to get them to do good work. The immature, however, needs to be both praised and scolded from time to time.

NEWS FLASH:

A close associate of Osama Bin Laden, Mohammad Afroz, who is currently in the high security Bombay prison, was involved in the plan to blow up a London airport. He took the Art of Living prison program and was totally transformed. He wrote that he wished all Al Qaeda members would do the course that brought forth such a transformation in him. His desire is to become an Art of Living teacher and bring peace and harmony to people!

23. BUSINESS AND SPIRITUALITY

FEBRUARY 2, 2002

NEW YORK, NEW YORK, UNITED STATES

Often spiritual people look down upon business, and spirituality is discarded as being impractical by businesspeople. The ancient people conceived spirituality as the heart, and business as the limbs. An individual or a society is incomplete without both these aspects.

Business brings material comfort, and spirituality brings mental and emotional comfort. Spirituality brings ethics and fair practice to business.

In the body-mind complex, depriving either the body or the mind of comfort means depriving both of them comfort.

You can't talk of spirituality to the poorest of the poor without taking care of their basic needs. They need to be supported materially. There's no spirituality in the world that's devoid of service, and service can't happen if material needs are ignored. Service can't happen only through the lips—you need legs. Love and compassion translated into action becomes service.

Every system has its flaws. Capitalism exploits the poor, while socialism dampens individual creativity and entrepreneurial spirit. Spirituality is the bridge between socialism and capitalism.

Spirituality gives the capitalist the heart to serve and the socialist the spirit to innovate.

NEWS FLASH:

While Gurudev attended the World Economic Forum in New York, the Art of Living Foundation was simultaneously being represented at the World Social Forum in Brazil and the UN Conference on Sustainable Development, also in New York.

24. STRENGTH AND SUBORDINATION

MARCH 30, 2001

RISHIKESH, INDIA

Many people don't want to work under someone else, be it in their profession, a company, or even when volunteering. The general notion is that when you work under someone, you lose your freedom—you have to be accountable.

Hence, many people choose to start their own business, wanting to be their own boss. But, in your own business, you're accountable to so many people. If you can't be accountable to even one person, how can you be accountable to many? This is the paradox. In fact, owning a business binds you more than having a boss!

Refusing to work under someone is a sign of weakness, not strength. A strong person will feel comfortable working under anyone because he knows his strength. It's the weak and poor in spirit who don't like to work under someone else, because they're unaware of their strength. They can't be successful in business or in any profession.

And the same is true even in the field of social service—often volunteers don't want to work under someone else. This is merely an exhibition of their weakness. With such an attitude, they achieve very little.

Someone who's timid and weak in spirit is uncomfortable working even under a wise person, but one who knows his own strength can work effectively even under a fool!

> *Audience member*: But to work under a fool is frustrating!
>
> *Gurudev*: When you know your strength, with skill and intelligence, you can turn every disadvantage into an advantage. A fool can bring out the best of your communication skills! (*Laughter*)

So, watch out! If you feel uncomfortable working under someone, it clearly shows you need to strengthen yourself.

Desiring freedom from circumstances or people is no freedom at all. Knowing that nobody can take away your freedom—that is strength! And when you realize your strength is unshakable, you'll not mind working under anybody.

NEWS FLASH:

More than a thousand people, including the royal family, took part in a charity walk in Muscat, Oman, to benefit the Art of Living 5H Program: Homes, Healthcare, Hygiene, Human Values, and Harmony in Diversity.

25. RELIGION AND POLITICS

JUNE 23, 1999

EAST DOVER, NOVA SCOTIA, CANADA

The role of religion is to make one righteous and loving, and politics means caring for people and their welfare. When religion and politics don't coexist, you have corrupt politicians and pseudo-religious leaders.

A religious man, who is righteous and loving, will definitely care for the welfare of the whole population and hence becomes a true politician. And a true politician can only be righteous and loving.

Figures such as Buddha, Krishna, and Christ, as well as prophets of all faiths, have been caring for people and have brought values to politics. You can find many examples of this.

Religions become unsuitable for creating a harmonious society when they restrict the freedom to worship or the modes of worship. When religion becomes all-encompassing and gives full freedom to pray and worship in any manner, it brings righteousness and peace and will be suitable for any society.

People think politics and religion have to be kept separate because many religions did not give freedom to worship and did not care for all people equally. History has shown that religion has created conflict. But irreligious societies have created chaos and corruption.

Today both religion and politics need reform. Religion has to become broader and more spiritual to allow freedom of worship and to encompass all the wisdom in the world. And politicians have to become more righteous and spiritual.

26. THE WISDOM OF SECRETS

DECEMBER 16, 1999

BANGALORE ASHRAM, INDIA

A wise person makes no effort to conceal a secret. But he doesn't make an effort to reveal a secret either. For example, you don't talk about menstruation or death to five-year-olds, but as they grow older, these things aren't hidden from them anymore. They become known as a matter of course.

An unenlightened one tries to protect a secret, which causes anxiety and discomfort. He also reveals the secret at the wrong time, to the wrong person, in the wrong place, and makes a big fuss about secrets.

An ignorant one is uncomfortable with a secret, whether revealed or unrevealed. But the wise one is comfortable with a secret, whether revealed or unrevealed.

When a worldly person tells you a secret, it will only create doubts and spread malaise.

When a wise person tells you a secret, it will uplift your consciousness and spread benevolence.

NEWS FLASH:

Prominent leaders of the Jain community are meeting in the Bangalore Ashram to discuss nonviolence on the 2,600th anniversary of the birth of Mahavira (a great teacher in Jainism).

27. TECHNOLOGY

AUGUST 3, 2000
EUROPEAN ASHRAM, BAD ANTOGAST, GERMANY

The purpose of technology is to harness nature to bring information and comfort to human beings. But when spiritual or human values are ignored and neglected, technology brings fear and destruction.

Technology without human values considers nature as inanimate. Science gives insight into the life of nature, and spirituality makes nature come alive.

Technology without spirituality can be destructive.

NEWS FLASH:

The first Art of Living course was held in Kosovo.

In Hanover, Germany, at Expo 2000, Gurudev was welcomed at the India Pavilion with much fanfare, including Aarti (a traditional Indian ceremony of respect) and regional dance. Accompanied by the melodious strains of a harp, he held a powerful meditation and spoke on the theme of the Expo: Humankind-Nature-Technology.

28. ARE YOU A TOURIST OR A PILGRIM?

NOVEMBER 3, 2000
JAMSHEDPUR, INDIA

What's the difference between a tourist and a pilgrim?

Both are on a journey.

A tourist satisfies the senses, whereas a pilgrim is on a quest for truth.

A tourist gets tired and tanned, while a pilgrim sparkles with spirit.

A pilgrim moves with sacredness and gratitude, while a tourist is often preoccupied and unaware.

A tourist compares his journey with other experiences and places and may not be in the present moment. But a pilgrim has a sense of sacredness, so he tends to be in the present moment.

Most people in life are just tourists without even being aware of it. Only a few make their life a pilgrimage.

Tourists come, look around, take pictures in their minds, only to come back again. But pilgrims are at home everywhere—they are centered in the Self.

When you consider life as sacred, the universe takes care of you.
Are you a tourist or a pilgrim?

29. THE OTHER SIDE OF FRIENDLINESS

JANUARY 31, 2001
FROM DAVOS TO ZURICH, SWITZERLAND

Secretaries, police, judges, accountants, and people in key positions shouldn't be friendly!

The main disadvantages of being friendly are:

- You come under obligation.

- You lose your freedom.

- Your perception can't be free and fair.

- Your thoughts and actions may not be impartial.

- Your focus, commitment, creativity, and, above all, your time will be wasted.

- You become prone to picking up bad habits and negative moods.

It takes wisdom to be free from the burden of obligation and not be influenced by your friends' opinions and feelings.

On many occasions, it's better to be unfriendly than friendly. Being unfriendly doesn't mean being aggressive and hostile. The best secretaries, personal assistants, security personnel, and judges have to be unfriendly.

Those who are aloof and indifferent get centered more quickly than those who are too friendly. A certain degree of reserve in every relationship will strengthen your personality and connect you to your source.

NEWS FLASH:

Gurudev was invited to the World Economic Forum in Switzerland to participate in a dialogue with other spiritual and religious leaders from the Vatican, Israel, Egypt, Bosnia, South Africa, France, and the United Kingdom.

Gurudev was the guest of honor at a reception hosted by a leading media magnate of Europe. In his welcoming speech, the host congratulated Gurudev and praised his beautiful energy.

Other dignitaries who attended the reception included ex-prime minister of Israel, Shimon Peres, British musician Peter Gabriel, renowned mountaineer Reinhold Messner, and CEO of Dell Computers, Michael Dell, as well as members of the European royalty and CEOs of Fortune 500 companies.

In the jam-packed hall, Gurudev was the center of attraction, as all the guests lined up to greet him personally. Several guests were heard commenting that they could feel Gurudev's energy in every corner of the room!

In India, hundreds of Art of Living volunteers are busily engaged in the relief efforts in the state of Gujarat. Within hours of the earthquake, our volunteers provided shelter and food to 1,500 people. Our satsang groups are arranging food, clothing, water, and funds.

30. CELEBRATE LIFE

MARCH 13, 1997

NEW DELHI, INDIA

Feeling that you're in a crowd when you're alone is ignorance. Enlightenment is feeling alone—"all one"—in a crowd, a feeling of oneness with the crowd— this is a sign of wisdom.

Some only know how to celebrate when they're in a crowd; some can only rejoice alone in silence. I tell you to do both.

Knowledge of life brings confidence, and knowledge of death (awareness of your own mortality) makes you fearless and centered.

> *Celebrate while you're alone and celebrate when you're with people.*
> *Celebrate the silence and celebrate the noise.*
> *Celebrate life and celebrate death.*

NEWS FLASH:

At an Ahmedabad sports stadium, eight thousand people joined together into one big satsang with Gurudev.

In Delhi, the capital of India, billboards announcing the event were seen at every major intersection. The stirring satsang and meditation captivated thousands.

31. PRESTIGE AND BEING HONORED—YOUR GOLDEN CAGE

MAY 3, 2001

PANAMA CITY, PANAMA

Being honored by others reduces freedom. Your virtue, good reputation, and fame can limit your freedom.

Nobody expects a good person to make a mistake. So the better you are, the higher the expectations people have of you. It's then that you lose your freedom. Your virtues and good deeds are like a golden cage. You're trapped by them, for everyone expects more from a good person, and nobody expects anything from a bad one.

Most people are stuck in this cage of prestige and good reputation. They can't smile from the heart or be natural. They're constantly worried about keeping up their prestige and their good reputation. It becomes more important than their own life. Just being good or doing good to retain prestige and a good reputation is worthless. Often, prestige and being honored can bring more misery in life than poverty.

Many desire fame, but little do they know that they're looking for a cage.

Only the wise know the art of being dignified and yet not becoming suffocated by it. For the wise, it's natural to be honored, but the wise person is not affected, even if it falls apart. Despite having fame or prestige, a wise person lives as though he or she has none. A wise person can handle any amount of fame without feeling suffocated, for he or she is crazy—unconcerned with the norms of society!

By doing good in society, one gains prestige. Then when enjoying the prestige and honors, one's freedom is lost.

> *Question*: Then how do you keep your freedom?
>
> *Gurudev*: By being like a child, considering the world as a dream, a burden, or a joke.

To be continued . . .

NEWS FLASH:

The state assembly of Sao Paulo in Brazil honored Gurudev after he spoke and conducted a group meditation. In Argentina, Gurudev addressed the prestigious International Council for Cultural Relationships and then moved on to Panama City, where he addressed a group of women government and business leaders and had private meetings with the mayor, the provincial governor, and the vice president.

32. LIFE IS A DREAM, A BURDEN, OR A JOKE

MAY 10, 2001

MONTREAL ASHRAM, CANADA

Often when you're happy, you feel life is a dream because you don't believe in the reality of it.

When there's misery, you feel life is a burden and take trivial things very seriously.

Yet one who's really gone through pleasure realizes that pleasure is also a burden. And if you've undergone misery thoroughly, you'll realize you've been guided or carried through it. When this realization comes, you feel life is a dream.

In between the extremes of pain and pleasure, life is like a joke.

> *Question*: What about life is like a joke?
>
> *Gurudev*: You don't question a joke. If you question a joke, it's no longer a joke. Don't question a burden either; it's a waste of time to question life and its events.

A burden makes you go deep. It gets you to the core of yourself. Realization of a dream wakes you up. And seeing life as a joke makes you light.

Life is very uncertain. Before it takes you away, realize that life is a dream, a burden, or a joke. Only when you realize this can you be centered.

NEWS FLASH:

Art of Living teachers gave a dynamic presentation about the Art of Living prison program and youth program to the Los Angeles Association of School Psychologists conference in Los Angeles.

33. ENLIGHTENMENT

MAY 21, 1996

BANGALORE ASHRAM, INDIA

Sometimes the question comes up, "What's the use of all these meditation courses if someone's behavior doesn't change?"

The spiritual knowledge acquired by a human being can't be measured or judged by external behavior. Some people may behave as though they've absorbed all the knowledge, but internally they haven't. The reverse is also true. Someone who seems not to have changed at all may have absorbed quite a lot.

Generally, people just look at external behavior, but the intelligent one looks beyond behavior and is amazed by the play of the formless, eternal, all-pervading one consciousness.

34. FOOLS WILL MAKE YOU WISER

JULY 17, 1996

GERMAN ACADEMY, BAD ANTOGAST, GERMANY

Respect everybody as you respect your spiritual teacher, but don't expect from everyone what you expect from your spiritual teacher.

You do it the other way. You don't respect everybody as you respect your teacher, but you expect them to give you joy and behave ideally. When they don't live up to your expectations, you get frustrated and you blame or curse them. By cursing, you lose your spiritual energy. Blessing brings your spiritual energy up.

The world is full of differences, and arguments are inevitable. With patience and wisdom, skillfully make your way.

If you find fools around you, know they're going to make you wiser. The number of fools around you indicates the strength of your centeredness. Don't try to get rid of them! (*Laughter*)

If you're not centered, you'll have no patience to put up with them. When you're totally established in the Self, you find the fools come up with wisdom. They're your own reflection; there's no "other." Fools offer you frustration and wisdom and make your life juicy.

> *Question*: How can you stop thinking others are fools?
>
> *Gurudev*: You don't have to. You can see the whole world as fools. The advantage is you don't get too attached to anyone. (*Laughter*)

No one likes to associate with fools. If you think people are sane, you want to join them.

You can think everybody is a fool and be cool.

NEWS FLASH FROM WASHINGTON, D.C.:

An Art of Living teacher, who is also a talented flautist, opened the Interfaith Prayer and Meditation Conference with a beautiful hallelujah bhajan, and everyone joined in. Children sang traditional devotional songs, and delegates from many faiths lit candles, offered deeply felt prayers, sang sweet hymns, and led the group in meditation. Represented faiths included the African Methodist Episcopal Church, Baha'i, Buddhism, Church of Christ, Presbyterian, Islam, Sufism, the Unity Church, Freemasons, Hinduism, and Sikh, among others.

35. THE PERSONAL AND THE IMPERSONAL

JUNE 25, 1997

MONTREAL ASHRAM, CANADA

When you love something, you make it personal. You raise the object to life. For children, everything is personal. Children take each object they play with and make it totally personal. Even a stone has a face; even the sun laughs.

When you attach emotion, the whole creation becomes personal.

When you remove the emotion, even people become objects.

Violence is removing the emotion. How can a person kill another person? It's when they don't see them as a person; they see them as an object. But even a stone attracts reverence when it becomes personal.

The impersonal can't attract reverence. Most people see God as impersonal and so they don't progress.

> *Question*: When we say something isn't real, then it's impersonal. When we personalize something, we make it real. So then, what is reality?
>
> *Gurudev*: You are the Reality. You're not the thoughts; you're not the emotions or actions. You're not really even a person . . . !
>
> *Exercise: What you now see as impersonal, see it as personal. And when you feel any negative emotion towards anybody, see them as impersonal.*

36. SHYNESS AND SHAME

AUGUST 22, 1996

35,000 FEET ABOVE THE ATLANTIC OCEAN

Shyness is associated with modesty, while shame accompanies ego. The body language in both shyness and shame is similar. However, one adds beauty to your expression, and the other brings guilt and is harmful to your health.

See how children are endowed with shyness; it's natural to them. Shame, however, is inflicted by society and is acquired. We shouldn't confuse timidity with modesty.

You should overcome shyness when it comes to expressing your abilities. At the same time, don't be shameless—it's good to be ashamed of doing wrong things.

Retain your shyness and let go of your shame. In letting go, the head bends and meets the heart.

NEWS FLASH:

Gurudev gave four television interviews on this tour, including shows for the Discovery Channel and Korean TV. Before boarding the plane to the United Kingdom, he took forty people to the amusement park for water rides and fun on the roller coaster.

37. UNCERTAINTY

DECEMBER 10, 1999

BANGALORE ASHRAM, INDIA

You can be at ease with the uncertainty of the world when you realize the certainty of the one infinite consciousness. Usually, people do just the opposite. They are certain about the things in the world and uncertain about God. They rely on something unreliable and get upset. Uncertainty causes craving for stability, and the most stable thing in the universe is the Self.

The world is changing; the Self is non-changing. Rely on the non-changing and accept the changing. If you're certain that everything is uncertain, you're liberated, free.

Uncertainty without the awareness of the Self makes you worried and tense. Uncertainty with the awareness of the Self brings higher states of consciousness and a smile.

People think that certainty is freedom. If you feel the freedom when you're uncertain, *that* is "real" freedom.

Often your certainty or uncertainty is based on the ever-changing world. When you're *certain* about the *uncertainty* of the changing world, it makes you *certain* about the existence of the non-changing reality underlying it. This brings a "certain" faith.

> *Question*: Can we still be enthusiastic when we are uncertain?
>
> *Gurudev*: Yes. In wisdom, you can be enthusiastic and act even in uncertainty. Often people who are uncertain about the Self are afraid. They don't act—they sit and wait. Acting in uncertainty makes life a game, a challenge. Agreeing to be in uncertainty is letting go.

38. SUCCESS

JUNE 2, 1999
OSLO, NORWAY

> *Question*: How was yesterday's program? Was it successful?
>
> *Gurudev*: There's no question of success if you have nothing to gain.

There's nothing to gain if you've only come to give and serve.

What does success mean? Success means crossing a limit, which shows you've assumed that you have a limit. Assuming a limit is underestimating yourself. If you're limitless, then there's no success. You don't say that you successfully drank a glass of water because it's well within your capabilities. But when you do something beyond your perceived limits, you claim success.

People running after success only exhibit their limitations. When you realize your unlimited nature, no action is an achievement.

If you claim to be successful, it only reveals your limitation and that you've underestimated yourself. All your gains can only be smaller than you. Taking pride in any gains is belittling yourself.

> *Question*: What if you feel that you're not serving successfully?
>
> *Gurudev*: When you serve others, you may feel that you haven't done enough, but you won't feel that you've been unsuccessful. Real service is when you feel that you haven't done enough.

NEWS FLASH:

The Scandinavian whirlwind tour started with lively satsangs in Denmark and Finland.

In Sweden, Swedish television filmed Gurudev for one hour for a millennium program. In Stockholm, Gurudev gave an entertaining talk with many humorous moments and, as usual, the best talks were not recorded.

Then it was on to the land of the midnight sun, Norway. More than two hundred diplomats and officials attended the Human Values Conference in Oslo, followed by a grand celebration in a beautiful hall.

39. PERFECTION IS THE NATURE OF THE ENLIGHTENED

OCTOBER 12, 2000

BANGALORE ASHRAM, INDIA

In a state of ignorance, imperfection is natural, and perfection is an effort.

In a state of wisdom or enlightenment, imperfection is an effort, but perfection is inevitable and unavoidable.

In that state of enlightenment, perfection means taking total responsibility, and total responsibility means seeing yourself as the only responsible person in the whole world. When you think that others are responsible, then your degree of responsibility may diminish.

When you're totally centered, you take care of even trivial and insignificant things with perfection.

40. THE PARADOX OF SACRIFICE

MARCH 15, 2001

RISHIKESH, INDIA

All the scriptures of the world glorify sacrifice. What is sacrifice?

It's giving up something that you value. You can only sacrifice that which you'd like to keep for yourself, in other words, that which gives you pleasure and joy. You can't sacrifice something that you dislike or reject.

Sacrifice is always related to a higher cause for a greater good. At the same time, when your love for the greater good is so strong, nothing else assumes any value. Sacrifice here becomes irrelevant because love alone is your strongest driving force.

So, when there's so much love, there can't be sacrifice. And when there's no love, there's no sacrifice.

For example, if a mother has made plans to see a movie and realizes that her child's sick, she doesn't say that she's sacrificed the movie to nurse her child. She simply didn't want to go since nothing else matters as much to her as being with her child.

You don't sacrifice something for someone you're in love with. When the love is lukewarm, *then* something appears to be a sacrifice.

Sacrifice purifies the human mind and reins in selfish tendencies. Yet sacrifice can also bring pride, arrogance, self-pity, and sometimes even depression.

You can sacrifice only that which you value. For a wise person, nothing is more precious than truth, values, and the Divine, and that person will never sacrifice those. This is the paradox of sacrifice.

NEWS FLASH:

Thousands got together in forty-three cities all over the world to participate in the 5H Walk for Gujarat to rehabilitate the earthquake-destroyed areas of Gujarat, India. It was well covered by the media.

Pakistan is the latest addition to the list of countries where Art of Living courses are conducted, bringing the total to 113.

41. COMMITMENT AND CONVENIENCE

APRIL 5, 2001

BALI, INDONESIA

A commitment can only be felt when it oversteps convenience. That which is convenient isn't commitment. If you just go by your convenience, your commitment falls apart, causing more inconvenience! If you keep dropping your commitment because it's inconvenient, can you be comfortable?

Often, what is convenient doesn't bring comfort but gives an illusion of comfort. Also, if you're too stuck in commitment, and it's inconvenient too often, you won't be able to fulfill your commitment, and it will cause frustration.

Wisdom is to strike a balance between convenience and commitment because both bring comfort to the body, mind, and spirit.

However, a seeker of knowledge should forget about convenience, so should soldiers, rulers, students, seekers of wealth, and all essential service providers.

Those who want to be creative and adventurous transcend convenience. Those who are ambitious and have a passion for a goal don't care for convenience. To the wise, commitment is their comfort. Whenever their commitment is shaken, their comfort is also shaken. Yet for the lazy, commitment is a torture though it's the best remedy.

Commitment will always bring comfort in the long run.

> *Question*: Are there any commitments that can be given up?
>
> *Gurudev*: Yes. Sometimes when you're committed without a vision, you feel stifled when your vision expands. Such commitments made with shortsightedness can be given up.
>
> - A smaller, less important commitment can be given up for a greater commitment.
> - Commitment to the means can be given up for the sake of the commitment to the goals.
> - When your commitment brings misery to many in the long run, it can be given up.

42. SELF-CONFIDENCE AND AMBITION

APRIL 17, 2001

HAWAII, UNITED STATES

Ambition indicates a lack of self-confidence!

When you know you can achieve something easily, you're not ambitious about it; you're simply confident that you can do it. Your ambition indicates challenge and uncertainty, which is contrary to self-confidence.

So, one who has total self-confidence can't be ambitious!

At the same time, a person who lacks total self-confidence can't be ambitious either!

And it's next to impossible to have total confidence without Self-knowledge. People take pride in being ambitious. The wise man will only smile at them. Ambition can never be for something you know you can achieve effortlessly. You can only be ambitious about something for which you must put forth effort, which poses a challenge, and which you're not even certain you'll be able to achieve.

Moreover, ambition takes away the joy of the moment.

With the knowledge of the Self, there's nothing left to achieve, for the entire existence is a mere play and display of one's own consciousness.

Also, with Self-knowledge, nothing is challenging to you, nor do you need to exert any effort. Nature is ready to fulfill your intentions even before they arise, not giving you a chance to crave or desire.

Nature doesn't allow the wise to have desires or ambitions, nor does it allow the unwise to always fulfill or get rid of them.

Do you still want to be ambitious, or is your only ambition to get rid of ambition? (*Laughter*)

NEWS FLASH:

Gurudev is encouraging satsang groups to read the Yoga Vasistha, an ancient Vedic text on the nature of consciousness.

43. DOING TRIVIAL THINGS

MAY 24, 2001

KODAIKANAL, INDIA

What can you do for eternity? Definitely not anything that's big or great, because it needs effort, and effort tires you. So, doing something great is a temporary state. If you can think of one thing that's well below your capacity to do and agree to do it for eternity, that becomes *puja* (sacred action).

The readiness to consciously do trivial things for eternity unites you with eternity. A simple act like observing a butterfly, watering the garden, watching the birds or the sky can bring deep relaxation, and relaxation connects you with your source. This is an antidote to ego. Ego is always ambitious and wants to do the toughest job, such as scaling the highest peak.

Not that you should do trivial things all your life, but consciously agreeing to do the trivial actions for eternity opens a new dimension and brings immense peace and restfulness.

To find rest in activity, choose an activity that's far below your capacity and agree to do it for all eternity. Doing a job far below your capacity and being satisfied with it will make it possible to do a job much beyond your capacity.

Know that all actions are born out of infinity, and that which is born out of infinity can take you to infinity.

44. AUTHENTICITY AND STRATEGY

JUNE 27, 2001

WASHINGTON, D.C., UNITED STATES

Being authentic and being strategic appear to be contradictory, but in fact they're complementary. Your intentions need to be authentic, and your actions need to be strategic. The more authentic the intention, the more strategic and skillful the action will be. Authentic intention and strategic action make you unshakable.

Yet strategy without authenticity makes you shallow. You can't have an authentic action and a strategic intention. If you try to be authentic in your action but manipulative in your mind, that's when mistakes happen.

Question: Is it possible to have a powerful intention, like greed, that's authentic?

Gurudev: If your intention is colored by such feelings as greed or over-ambition, then your intention is not authentic. Whenever your intentions are impure, it pricks your conscience, so it can't be authentic. Authentic intentions are free from negative emotions. An action that's not skillful leads to negative emotions, and an intention that's not authentic harbors negative emotions.

Question: If our intention is authentic and yet our actions are not skillful, what should we do?

Gurudev: Carry a handkerchief and get ready for tears! (*Laughter*)

Question: What's the best skill to deal with intention?

Gurudev: Don't keep any intentions to yourself. Offer them to the Higher Self.

Actions can never be perfect, but our intentions can be perfect. Actions always have room for improvement. Action means growth and movement, and that needs space.

The depth and the freedom in you bring out the skillfulness in you.

NEWS FLASH:

Gurudev ended the East Coast portion of his tour at the historic Constitution Hall on the National Mall in Washington, D.C., just one block from the White House.

45. THE STRENGTH OF COMMITMENT

APRIL 27, 2002
BOSTON, MASSACHUSETTS, UNITED STATES

Question: Why is it easier for some of us to commit to our own welfare rather than that of others?

Gurudev: Because you don't know that whatever you're committed to brings you strength.

If you're committed to your family, then your family supports you. If you're committed to society, you enjoy the support of society. If you're committed to truth, truth brings you strength.

Often people aren't aware of this, and that's why they're hesitant to commit to a greater cause. There's also a fear that commitment will take away their freedom. Your commitment to a cause is bound to bring you comfort in the long run. The higher the commitment, the greater the good for all.

When the path is charming, commitment is effortless and is part of your nature.

> *Audience member*: That's why in the Art of Living we don't take vows; we have wows! (*Laughter*)

NEWS FLASH:

Gurudev's visit to Saarbrucken and Stutgaart in Germany was extensively covered by the media. Three more universities in Berlin have made the Art of Living course a part of their curriculum, for a total of five universities officially offering the course.

46. TWO TYPES OF HAPPINESS

Happiness and success both depend on our ability to give. There are two types of happiness: one is in taking, and the other is in giving.

A child enjoys taking things. When you take children to a toy store, that's it! They want to bring the whole toy store home. They like to grab everything. This is an infant's happiness.

Then there's a happiness that's more mature. That's the happiness you get from giving. For example, when you're at home by yourself, you don't usually make a big meal. But when friends or family come, you prepare many types of dishes and take joy in feeding them. This is a mature joy, which comes from giving because there is a joy in giving.

Around the world, you'll find many people who enjoy giving. Why do they give? They give because giving gives them more joy. Giving gives you happiness that's unparalleled.

A successful person is one who has tasted the joy that comes from giving and keeps on giving. This is the sign of success. And it's not the object you give that matters, but the attitude of sharing.

Happiness is when you want nothing, and you want to give. At the precise point where wanting and desires end and sharing begins, that's where happiness can be found.

47. KNOWLEDGE TIDBITS

Question: What should you do if your commitment is boring?

Gurudev: Commitment has value when things are not so charming. When things are interesting, you don't need commitment at all. You never say you're committed to doing something that's very interesting or charming.

Question: What's the best way to learn?

Gurudev: Learning is inevitable. By doing things right, you learn, and by doing things wrong, you also learn. From every situation, from everybody, you learn either what to do or what not to do. Either by committing mistakes or by doing things correctly, you can't help but learn.

In deep slumber, you don't learn. And if you're asleep in your life, there's neither pain nor pleasure nor learning.

Question: How do I improve my patience?

Gurudev: Can I tell you next year? (*Laughter*)

Question: How do I improve my memory?

Gurudev: Ask me this question later! (*Laughter*)

Question: If you have a spiritual teacher, do you still need luck?

Gurudev: You need luck to have a spiritual teacher! (*Laughter*)

Chasing Happiness:
The Nature of Desires

1. DESIRE AND JOY

MARCH 6, 1996

BANGALORE ASHRAM, INDIA

All desires are for happiness. That's the goal of every desire, isn't it? Yet how often does your desire lead you to that goal? Desires when fulfilled give rise to more desires.

Have you thought about the nature of desire? It simply means joy tomorrow and not now, doesn't it?

But joy is never tomorrow. It's always experienced now.

When you're joyful, how can you have desires? And how can you be joyful when you are in the grip of desire?

Desire promises to lead you to happiness. In fact, it can't. And that's why it's *maya* (delusion).

2. DEALING WITH DESIRES

MARCH 20, 1996

SWARGASHRAM (HEAVENLY ABODE), RISHIKESH, INDIA

Desires arise on their own, don't they? Do they ask you before they come? And when they come, what do you do with them? If you don't want to have any desires, then that itself is another desire.

Now here's a clue for you:

If you want to get on a plane or go to a movie, you have to buy a ticket. This ticket needs to be given at the door. If you hold on to the ticket, how will you go in?

If you want to be admitted to a college, you must fill out an application form and then submit it—you can't hold on to it.

On the journey of life, you have to keep submitting your desires and not hold on to them. And as you keep submitting them, fewer desires come up.

> *Unfortunate are those who keep on desiring, yet their desires aren't fulfilled.*
>
> *A little more fortunate are those whose desires get fulfilled, but over a long period of time.*
>
> *More fortunate are those whose desires get fulfilled as soon as they arise.*
>
> *The most fortunate are those who have no desires because there's fulfillment before a desire can arise.*

3. THREE TYPES OF HAPPINESS

The most basic trait of human nature is to seek happiness. It's amazing to see to what extent a person will go to find happiness. In reality, happiness comes from within, but most people seek it outside. While the senses can give pleasure, the soul yearns for something more. This impulse of seeking is the beginning of one's spiritual journey.

There are three types of happiness.

The first type of happiness is not so enjoyable to begin with, but always leads to joy. The happiness that comes from self-discipline is really long-lasting happiness.

The second type of happiness starts with enjoyment but ends in suffering. Such happiness is no happiness at all.

The third type of happiness just appears to be enjoyable but is actually misery from beginning to end.

Unfortunately, many people are tempted to take shortcuts in their quest for joy and end up in addiction. Drugs seem to give a high, and people say they take drugs to experience an altered state of consciousness. However, over time, the aftereffects can leave the system totally shattered. The aspiration to find freedom, love, and happiness leaves these people with bondage, despondency, and misery. When having something is not joyful, but *not* having it is painful—this is the state of addiction.

Chasing short-term joy leads to long-term misery, and it is spiritual education alone that gives the wisdom to choose slight discomfort in the short-term to have lasting happiness in the long run.

4. ALWAYS?

NOVEMBER 4, 1999

BANGALORE ASHRAM, INDIA

How can you always be happy? Forget about "always"; then you'll be happy.

In always wanting to be comfortable, one becomes lazy. In always wanting perfection, one becomes angry. In always wanting to be rich, one becomes greedy.

Fear comes when we don't realize that only life is for always. This projection of the nature of Self (which is "always") onto the temporal (which can never be "always") is called *maya* (delusion).

If you remove "always" from your vocabulary, then everything is "all right." Drop "always," and all will be right—that's intelligence.

NEWS FLASH:

Gurudev was the chief guest at a Muslim gathering held in India, where he spoke on "Human Values and the Prophet Mohammed."

Gurudev initiated a revolutionary movement among twenty-four prominent saints of India to welcome His Holiness Pope John Paul II to India, an event that was publicized in several national newspapers.

5. DESIRES AND WAKING UP

All desires arise when your mind is not fully conscious. A semiconscious mind is the mother of desires. When the mind is completely unconscious, no desire comes. For instance, in sleep there is no desire. And when the mind is fully awake, then also there is no desire.

What does desire mean? It means a lack of joy or fulfillment. It's not that desires should be stopped if they arise. When they're there, they're there. Desires don't ask your permission. They just drop in. Just take them as they come and don't hold on to them. Wanting to have no desires in life is also another desire.

When desires arise, wake up. Become more conscious and aware of your nature—you are joy.

6. ATTAINING EXPANDED AWARENESS

MARCH 25, 1999
RISHIKESH, INDIA

Desire, action, and the experience of expanded awareness are all manifestations of the same energy that's within you—and at any point in time, one of the three dominates.

When you have lots of desires, awareness will be at its lowest—that's why philosophers all around the world have always advocated renunciation and dropping of desires.

> *When desire dominates, you live in an imaginary world, and stress and sorrow result. When action dominates, unawareness, restlessness, and fatigue follow. When awareness is dominant, then happiness dawns.*

When your actions and desires are sincerely directed to the Divine or to the welfare of society, your consciousness is automatically elevated, and expanded awareness is sure to be attained.

7. DESIRE AND PRAYERFULNESS

NOVEMBER 20, 1996
CALCUTTA, INDIA

For your prayer to be answered, the desire has to be intense. The greater the intensity of desire and the longer it takes to get fulfilled, the greater the gratitude.

For desire to become intense, the passage of time and a feeling of need are required. Intense desire leads you to devotion.

When a desire is fulfilled, it loses its charm and significance in the overwhelming feeling of gratitude.

The son of a farmer in India had a lifelong desire to go to England, and he prayed deeply for it. When the news of his trip finally materialized, he was filled with such immense gratitude that he no longer cared whether he went or not.

Often people think they're unfortunate if their desires don't get fulfilled quickly. An intense desire can either frustrate you or make you prayerful. In prayerfulness, there's gratitude and devotion. Any intense experience makes you whole.

8. INTENTION

DECEMBER 23, 1999
EUROPEAN ASHRAM, BAD ANTOGAST, GERMANY

Intentions keep the tension in. Being deeply centered means dropping all intentions.

In tension, rest doesn't become deep. But love for the Divine dissolves intentions.

Intention pushes you to the future, yet bliss is always in the present. The one who wakes up to this truth is wise. Occasionally, if an intention arises in a state of bliss, it manifests effortlessly.

The more intentions you have, the more "in tension" you'll be. To minimize your intentions could be your last intention.

NEWS FLASH:

The Art of Living was invited to participate in the millennium celebration with the Dalai Lama at Varanasi.

9. TRUE JOY

Human life is a combination of body (matter) and spirit (vibration), isn't it? Pleasure or joy is forgetting that you're matter and becoming an intense vibration.

Carnal instincts also bring up intense vibrations momentarily, and that's how they give a glimpse of joy. But this joy is short-lived and makes you sink deeper into matter later on.

Pleasure that comes from satsang is of a higher nature. *Kirtan* (call-and-response chanting) and singing create vibrations in the spirit; that's why when you sing, the ecstasy stays for a long time.

Pleasure in the subtle is long-lasting, energizing, refreshing, and freeing. Pleasure from the surface level of life is short-lived, tiring, and binding.

When you know you're electricity (vibration/energy), then craving, greed, lust, and anger disappear—your life becomes a true celebration.

NEWS FLASH:

This week, Gurudev traveled to Chennai for a huge satsang. Then he went to Delhi, where he met with the vice president of India.

The Senses

1. FIRE

JULY 24, 1995
MONTREAL ASHRAM, CANADA

The senses are like fire. Whatever you put in the fire of your senses, burns.

The fire from toxic material creates pollution and a foul smell. But if you burn incense, it creates fragrance.

The same fire that supports life can also destroy it. A fire can heat your home or burn it down. Celebration often happens around a bonfire. In many cultures, grief happens around a fire of cremation.

Are you the fire that creates smoke and pollution or the flame that creates light and fragrance?

> *A saint creates light and the fragrance of love and is the friend of life.*
> *When your senses are engaged in goodness, then you'll create light.*
> *When engaged otherwise, you create misery for yourself and others.*

It is *sanyama* (self-discipline or commitment to good habits) that transforms the quality of fire in you. Next we will discuss *sanyama*.

2. BREAKING BAD HABITS

JULY 30, 1995
BROOKFIELD, CONNECTICUT, UNITED STATES

How to get rid of *vasanas* (negative thought patterns ingrained in the mind)? This is a question for all those who want to break bad habits.

You want to get rid of these habits because they give you pain and restrict you. The nature of a *vasana* is to bother you—bind you—and wanting to be free is the nature of life. When a soul does not know how to be free, it wanders, sometimes for lifetimes, craving freedom.

One way to release bad habits is by taking a "vow."

A vow should be time-bound. Suppose someone resolves to quit smoking and is unable to do it—he can take a time-bound vow not to smoke for five days. If someone is used to swearing, he can take a vow not to use bad language for ten days. Don't make a vow for a lifetime—you'll likely break it immediately! If you do happen to break it, don't worry—just begin again.

When you fulfill your vow, pick a new starting time and make the vow again. Gradually increase the length of your vow until it becomes your very nature.

This is *sanyama*—self-discipline. Everybody is endowed with some self-discipline.

When the mind falls back into its old patterns, you could be discouraged, blame yourself, and feel that you haven't made any progress. Or you could see it as an opportunity for *sanyama* and feel happy about it.

Bad habits will stop you from blossoming and drain your life energy. Without *sanyama*, life won't be happy and healthy. For example, you know you shouldn't overeat. If you do, you'll get sick. With the practice of self-discipline, you can give a positive direction to your life energy and rise above any habit.

Take a time-bound vow today and make a note of it. If you break a vow, make a note of it and share the time and date with a trusted friend. Make your vow again and keep going. Bind those habits that bring you pain in *sanyama*.

3. GIFT WRAP

JANUARY 11, 1996
WEGGIS, SWITZERLAND

All sensory pleasures in the world are like gift wrap; the true bliss is the present inside.

Divine love is that present, yet we hold on to the wrapping paper, believing we've already enjoyed the gift. It's like putting a piece of chocolate in your mouth with the wrapping still on. A little chocolate may seep onto your tongue, but the paper will cut your mouth.

Unwrap the present. The whole world is there for you to enjoy, but don't get lost in it. The wise know how to enjoy the gift inside, while the ignorant get stuck on the wrapping paper.

4. WINDOW SHUTTERS

AUGUST 13, 1997
STOCKHOLM, SWEDEN

To the degree that you're awake, everything around you brings knowledge. If you're not awake, even the most precious knowledge doesn't make any sense.

(Suddenly there was a lot of noise outside, and someone went to shut the window.)

> *Gurudev*: Awareness depends upon your ability to open and shut your "windows."
>
> When there's a storm, you need to shut your windows; otherwise you'll get wet. When it's hot and suffocating inside, you need to open your windows.
>
> Your senses are like windows. When you have the ability to open and shut your windows at will, then you're free and awake spiritually.
>
> If your senses can't be shut or opened at will—you're bound.
>
> Attending to this is *sadhana*, or spiritual practice.

NEWS FLASH:

In Copenhagen, Gurudev was featured on *Good Morning Denmark.*

Extensive media coverage of Gurudev's visit to Stockholm brought far more people for the evening program than could be accommodated. Gurudev first greeted those who could not get in—the last shall be first!

5. STIMULATING THE SOUL

JANUARY 26, 1999
EUROPEAN ASHRAM, BAD ANTOGAST, GERMANY

When a part of the body is stimulated, pleasure arises. When your soul is stimulated, love arises.

Pleasure ends, but love has no end. Often people think pleasure is love. The distinction between the two has to be understood. Only the fortunate will understand.

In the same way that sugar stimulates the tongue, music stimulates the ears and sight the eyes. What stimulates the soul? Meditation, wisdom, and the company of the enlightened!

All that one wants is the stimulation of the soul. Even a faint idea of it keeps life going. All other stimuli are on the surface. The stimulus of the soul energizes, and the stimulus of the body brings tiredness.

Every stimulus should lead you to the Self. So that when you listen to music, you transcend the music, and when you listen to knowledge, it takes you to silence.

6. THE NATURE OF THE FIVE SENSES IS KNOWLEDGE

DECEMBER 30, 1999
CARRARA, ITALY

Every cell in your body has the ability of all five senses. So each cell of the body has the potential to perform all the functions of the senses.

All cells are made of the same tissue—each DNA molecule contains all functions of the body. The five senses and the ability to think are all present in consciousness, which is inherent in all the cells.

Vision is part of consciousness. That's why in dreams, you can see without the eyes.

You can feel without the skin. That's why people without limbs can still feel sensations in their missing limbs.

You can smell without the nose and taste without the tongue.

When someone says something, you're "all ears"—you listen with every cell of your body. There's an expression in India, "looking with a thousand eyes"—one is all eyes.

Every sensory stimulus brings knowledge, which is the nature of consciousness. Knowing is the nature of consciousness.

> *Question*: Some people who have lost one of their senses find that the others become heightened.
>
> *Gurudev*: You don't have to lose one to sharpen the others. You can sharpen all of them in deep silence.

> *Exercise: Sit comfortably, easily, and close your eyes. Feel that every cell has the potential to see and hear. Know that you're all eyes, all ears.*

NEWS FLASH:

A huge Christmas tree adorned the meditation hall in the German Art of Living Academy for a beautiful Christmas celebration, complete with gifts of wisdom and grace.

The Massachusetts Institute of Technology (MIT) in Boston has introduced the Art of Living course as part of its curriculum.

Thirteen hundred people have assembled on the Mediterranean in an indoor stadium with Gurudev to celebrate and welcome the new millennium.

PART 3

MOVING FROM THE SMALL SELF TO THE BIG SELF AND BEYOND

Understanding Your Mind

1. FIVE FACTORS THAT INFLUENCE THE MIND

JANUARY 6, 2000

MILANO, ITALY

There are five factors that impact the mind: place, time, food, past experiences, and associations and actions.

Every place you are impacts the mind differently. You can feel this even in different rooms in your house. A place where there's singing and meditation has a different influence on the mind. Suppose you like a particular place. You may find that a little later, it won't be the same.

Time is also a factor. Different times of the day and year have different influences on the mind.

The food you eat has an effect on you that lasts for several days.

Your past experiences (and the *karmic* impressions resulting from them) also have an impact on the mind, coloring your experience of the present. Awareness, understanding, and meditation all help erase the influence of past experiences.

The people and events you're associated with and your own actions affect your mind. In certain company your mind behaves in one way and with others in a different way.

> *Question*: Should we worry about them?
>
> *Gurudev*: No need to be paranoid about it. Just know these factors.

Though these five factors influence life and the mind, know that your Higher Self is much more powerful. As you grow in knowledge and understanding, you'll influence them all.

NEWS FLASH:

Celebrations and New Year's silent retreats were held in ninety-three countries to welcome the new millennium.

In Tuscany, Italy, about 1,300 people from more than forty-one countries gathered to participate in the celebration and retreat being held there. As the sun set, everyone sat on the beach with Gurudev, chanting to say goodbye to the passing millennium. They were uplifted and inspired by a silent meditation at midnight and *kirtan* with songs in many languages. In fact, the retreat participants were so blissed out that the French translator spoke into the Italian earphones for forty minutes so the French had no translation, yet not one person complained!

A few days later, Gurudev spoke on Italian national television as part of the continuing celebration.

A dog story: There was a man who walked his dog every day for seven years. One afternoon, the dog pulled the leash out of the man's hand and ran away. The dog had never done this before!

After searching for ten minutes, the man saw the dog standing at the base of a pole. The man called the dog to him, but the dog wouldn't move—also something the dog had never done before.

As the man approached the dog, he noticed a poster on the pole. Grabbing the dog's leash, he was close enough to read the poster, which announced the New Millennium celebration with Gurudev in Milan. The man was immediately intrigued and decided he would attend and bring some friends. The man felt grateful to his dog for leading him and his friends to a chance for spiritual growth.

2. YOU AND YOUR TIME

APRIL 8, 1999
BANGALORE ASHRAM, INDIA

When you feel time is too short, you're either restless or in a state of expanded awareness. When you feel time is too long, you're either miserable or you have a keen mind.

When you are happy and when you love what you're doing, you don't feel the time. Similarly, during sleep, you don't feel time.

In deep meditation, you *are* time, and everything is happening within you; events are happening in you like clouds coming and going in the sky.

When you're ahead of time, planning for the future, events seem to drag and are boring. When time is ahead of you—things are happening too fast and you're lagging behind—you're surprised and shocked. You can't digest the events.

When you're with time, you're wise and at peace.

> *Exercise: Just observe yourself and see if you are managing time or time is managing you.*

NEWS FLASH:

During Gurudev's first visit to the mountain kingdom of Nepal, he was received at the airport by the prime minister's emissary and later had a meeting with the prime minister. An impressive meeting of dignitaries was followed by a joyful satsang of nearly three thousand people.

3. LETTING GO OF CONTROL

DECEMBER 27, 2001

EUROPEAN ASHRAM, BAD ANTOGAST, GERMANY

Many have a problem with letting go of control. This causes anxiety, restlessness, and soured relationships.

Wake up and see, are you really in control? What are you in control of? Perhaps a tiny part of your waking state! Isn't that so?

- You're not in control when you're sleeping or dreaming.
- You're not in control of the thoughts and emotions coming up in you. You may choose to express them or not, but they come to you without your prior permission!
- Most of the functions of your body aren't in your control.

If you think you're in control of all the events in your life, in the world, or in the universe—that's a joke!

When you look at things from this angle, you don't need to be afraid of losing control because you have none.

Whether you realize it or not, when you let go of your sense of control, that's when you truly relax. Your attachment to your identity and the roles you play doesn't let you totally relax and keeps you restricted.

4. WHICH IS MORE EXPENSIVE: YOUR SMILE OR YOUR ANGER?

SEPTEMBER 25, 1996

BANGALORE ASHRAM, INDIA

Usually, you give your anger freely and your smile rarely, as though a smile is costly. In ignorance, anger is cheaper, and a smile is costly. In wisdom, a smile is free—like sunshine, air, and water—and anger is extremely expensive, like a diamond.

Conclusion: Be generous with your smile and frugal with your anger.

5. TIME AND MIND

DECEMBER 10, 1997

BANGALORE ASHRAM, INDIA

When you're happy, the mind expands; time appears too short. When you're unhappy, the mind contracts; time appears too long.

When the mind experiences equanimity, you transcend time.

To escape from time, many resort to alcohol, drugs, sleep, etc., but when the mind is dull or unconscious, it's unable to experience the Self.

Samadhi (transcendence or going beyond the mind, timelessness) is the real peace. A few moments of *samadhi* gives the mind a lot of energy. This is the greatest healer.

Before you fall into a slumber and as soon as you wake up from sleep, in these moments of twilight in consciousness, experience timelessness beyond the mind!

NEWS FLASH:

In Apple Valley, California, eighty homeless children received gifts at a special Christmas party.

In the slums of Mumbai, India, satsangs and service projects have begun. A blood donation camp was organized in Surat. Some people in the villages surrounding the ashram were given free housing.

6. WONDER

What is the difference between asking a question and wonder? A question demands an answer, whereas wonder doesn't require an answer.

Questions are often associated with sorrow.

Wonder is associated with joy.

You never question "Why am I so happy? Why am I so beautiful? Why am I so good? Today I feel great! Why is that?" Instead you've just wondered. You've never expected an answer about being joyful. But when problems come, something's wrong, we ask, "Why does this happen to me?"

Enlightenment is not getting answers to questions. It is simply making a question into "a wonder." Any answer can bring ten more questions. Letting a question become a wonder brings freedom to the mind. The mind can relax.

7. ANNIHILATE CONFLICT

NOVEMBER 14, 1996
KUALA LUMPUR, MALAYSIA

When you're in a harmonious environment, your mind picks up any excuse to be in conflict. Often small things are enough to create a big turmoil. Have you noticed this?

When your survival is at stake, you don't complain that nobody loves you. But when you're safe and secure, you start demanding attention. Many people create conflict in order to get attention.

Ask yourself this question: Do I seek harmony in every situation, or do I seek to widen the differences and prove that I'm right?

The seed of negativity and the tendency for conflict in you can be annihilated only by sadhana *(spiritual practices).*

NEWS FLASH:

Gurudev addressed a group of medical professionals in the afternoon and religious leaders at an interfaith conference that evening. The Honorable Minister for Works attended the official launching of the Malaysian Art of Living Society.

8. EGO

NOVEMBER 20, 1997

BANGALORE ASHRAM, INDIA

Being in your ego creates an experience of separateness, a sense of not belonging, and wanting to prove and to possess. Ego causes heaviness, discomfort, fear, and anxiety. It restricts your genuine expression.

When is there ego?

1.   When you don't get attention.

2.   When you seem to be losing attention.

3.   When you get attention. (*Laughter*)

Ego doesn't let love flow. Ego can be transcended by knowing your true Self, by enquiring, "Who am I?"

Often, your attitude toward an egotistical person is one of contempt or jealousy. But since egotism comes from ignorance, you should have compassion, or even pity, don't you think so?

There's also a positive aspect of ego. It drives one to do some work. A person will do a job either out of compassion or out of ego. Most of the work in society is by boosting the ego. But in a spiritual setting, work is done out of love. And when you wake up and see that there is nothing to be proved and nothing to possess, ego dissolves.

9. BREAK THE BARRIER OF THE RATIONAL MIND

JUNE 10, 1998

NEW YORK, NEW YORK, UNITED STATES

You usually only do that which is purposeful, useful, and rational. Everything you see, you see through the rational mind.

But an intuition, a discovery, and new knowledge go beyond the rational mind. Truth is beyond reason.

The rational mind is like a railroad track that is fixed in grooves. Truth needs no tracks. Truth can float anywhere like a balloon.

Some people step out of the rational mind to rebel against society. They want to break social law, but it's for the sake of ego—out of anger, hatred, rebelliousness, and wanting attention. This isn't stepping out of the rational mind, though they may think so.

We step out of the rational mind when we do something that has no purpose. If there's no purpose, the action becomes a game. Life becomes lighter.

If you're stuck with only rational acts, life is a burden. But if you just drop the rational mind and act, if you play a game without a thought of winning or losing—doing something without any purpose attached to it—it's freedom, like a dance.

Just step out of the rational mind, and you'll find great freedom, an unfathomable depth, and you'll come face-to-face with reality.

Reality transcends logic and the rational mind. Until you transcend the rational mind, you won't get access to creativity, innovation, and the infinite.

But remember: If you do a non-rational act in order to find freedom, then you already have a purpose. It's no longer non-rational. (This note has already spoiled its own possibility!)

Break the barrier of the rational mind and find freedom for yourself.

NEWS FLASH:

In South Africa, Gurudev's talk made headline news in Johannesburg and Durban. Senior government officials and prominent religious leaders met Gurudev at our International Symposium on Human Values. The premier of the Kwa-Zulu Natal Province offered to organize Art of Living courses in the local prisons. Our International Association for Human Values 1998 Award was given to President Nelson Mandela. The African tour left crowds wanting more.

Gurudev moved on to crowds in Atlanta and New York, and tomorrow he will address the Values Caucus at the United Nations.

10. DROP YOUR SELF-IMAGE

MAY 7, 1997

MAURITIUS

Question: How can we make everyone happy?

Gurudev: Become centered.

Question: How do we become centered?

Gurudev: What restricts you and stands between you and being centered is your self-image. Your self-image, whether good or bad, causes misery.

When you think highly of yourself, in a subtle manner you judge others. Then feelings like anger, jealousy, and hatred follow.

When you think badly about yourself, you feel low, and again you start getting angry and hating everyone.

When you think highly of yourself, you're in trouble.
When you think badly about yourself, you're in greater trouble!
So drop your self-image.

NEWS FLASH:

The Malaysian silent retreat ended on Sunday, and the celebration moved on for the first time to the island country of Mauritius, off the East Coast of Africa. Three grand celebrations were held with filled halls. The prime minister and many cabinet ministers also came.

Gurudev gave a talk at the police headquarters to an attentive audience of two hundred police officers and the commissioner of police. Many ended up singing and afterward came up to hug Gurudev.

11. MEMORY

NOVEMBER 27, 1997

BANGALORE ASHRAM, INDIA

It is memory that makes you miserable or wise.

Memory of experiences and events in the ever-changing world, however good or bad, constricts the vastness of the Self—it binds you.

Memory of the non-changing Self expands and elevates awareness—it liberates you.

You are what you are, because of your memory.

If you're stressed and unhappy, it's because of your memory. If you're centered and free, it's also because of your memory.

Forgetfulness of the infinite is misery. Forgetfulness of the trivial is ecstasy.

> *Question*: How do we get rid of unpleasant memories and limitations?
>
> *Gurudev*: Just wake up and see that whatever has happened has happened, it's finished. Life is new every moment. Just focus on life right now, this very moment. Drop this questioning, "Oh, why did this happen this way? Why did it not happen that way?" There is nothing to gain by thinking about the past over and over again. Let it go!
>
> • Know the impermanent nature of the world and events.
>
> • Be dispassionate and centered.
>
> • Be in the company of the wise. In their presence, knowledge of the Self is gained.
>
> • Increase *prana* (life force energy).
>
> • And if none of this works, time will take care of it!

NEWS FLASH:

Gurudev was the chief guest of a congregation of the Lions Clubs of Karnataka, attended by many dignitaries, where several service projects were initiated.

A massive rally was organized for environmental awareness in Bangalore, followed by a huge satsang.

12. RESPECT AND EGO

DECEMBER 16, 2001

BANGALORE ASHRAM, INDIA

There are two types of respect:

1.   Respect that comes to you because of your position, fame, or wealth. This type of respect is impermanent. It can be lost once you lose your wealth or status.

2.   Respect that comes because of your virtues, such as honesty, kindness, commitment, and patience. No one can take away this kind of respect.

Yet when you get attached to your virtues, you look down on everybody else and your virtues start diminishing. Not being attached to virtues brings the highest self-respect.

Often ego is confused with self-esteem. Ego needs the other for comparison, but self-esteem is just confidence in oneself. A person claiming that they're skilled in mathematics or geography is an example of self-esteem. But to say, "I know better than everybody else," is ego.

Your ego will often upset you, while self-esteem makes you immune to getting upset from external factors. Ego demands respect, whereas the virtues in you command respect.

You can never get respect by demanding—you have to command it.

NEWS FLASH:

This time all roads did not lead to Rome, but to Florence, where people from all over Italy flocked to meet Gurudev. The governor of Tuscany, who has also done the Art of Living course and silent retreats, organized the program.

Then Gurudev arrived in Lithuania to inspire the assembly of East European teachers and lead a silent retreat.

13. THE MIND IS LIKE A SPIDER

All the silly little concerns the mind has—they become its own web. And the mind gets caught up in its own web, like the spider web. The spider, from its own saliva, makes its own web, gets caught up in its own web, and dies in its own web.

In the same way, the mind gets caught up in its own net, imagining its own events. It creates a whole trail of its imaginations and gets caught up in it. Wake up and see: "This is all of my own making." In that moment you become free. Absolutely free.

14. THE BEAUTIFUL "I DON'T KNOW"

The way of the wise is to see uncertainty with a sense of wonderment. Wonderment is the beginning of new knowledge. Creativity dawns by stretching, or expanding, wonder.

The attitude of "I know" closes you off and limits you, whereas "I don't know" makes way for new possibilities.

Often one says, "I don't know," out of frustration. Turning that upset "I don't know'" to an "I don't know" that comes with a sense of wonder is the path of growth. The more one knows, the more wonderment dawns about the unknown. It's said that what is known is not even the tip of the iceberg of the unknown.

15. THE OTHER SIDE OF EGO

MARCH 8, 2001
RISHIKESH, INDIA

Ego impedes a leader, a wise man, a merchant, or a servant, but it's necessary for a warrior or a competitor. A warrior is one who takes on challenges and commitments and stands by them.

Ego makes one sacrifice oneself for a cause. Ego gives strength and courage and brings valor to meet the challenges with perseverance. A strong ego will counteract depression. Often ego is considered selfish, but it's the greatest motivating factor for creativity and generosity.

Ego propels one to venture into the unknown.

In Vedic philosophy, there are three types of ego based on the three main qualities of creation—*sattvic* (joyful and serene), *rajasic* (restless, full of desires and ambitions), and *tamasic* (dull and negative).

1. *Tamasic* ego is barbaric and blind and has self-destructive tendencies.

2. *Rajasic* ego is self-centered and causes misery to oneself and others.

3. *Sattvic* ego is creative and has protective tendencies.

The latter is better than the two before it. Have a *sattvic* ego, as a *sattvic* ego is always ready to give and sacrifice for others.

NEWS FLASH:

So far, fifty truckloads of relief supplies have reached the areas severely hit by the earthquake in Gujarat. Our teachers are busy facilitating courses to help people deal with their trauma.

16. BLESSED ARE THOSE WHO ARE BORED

JUNE 16, 1999
ARENAL VOLCANO, TABACÓN, COSTA RICA

Only a conscious, alert, and dynamic person can get bored. A dull and lazy person doesn't get bored. If you get bored, it indicates you're more alive and human. It's a sign that you're growing, that you're evolving.

An animal, for example, keeps doing the same thing. It never gets bored. Cows, horses, and birds do the same things over and over all their lives.

People eat, watch television, change jobs, and change partners to escape boredom. And they get frustrated. Frustration takes them back to inertia and unconsciousness.

There are only two states where boredom does not occur: in a state of total inertia or in a state of Divine consciousness. If you are bored, it indicates you are evolving. Boredom moves you.

Audience member: Boredom moves you toward the Divine.

Gurudev: Yes, be proud of your boredom and celebrate!

NEWS FLASH:

In Panama, the warmth of the Latin American hearts and songs lit up the celebrations.

In Costa Rica, Gurudev had a diplomatic reception and a motorcycle escort, and his talk was cosponsored by the University of Peace and the National Commission for Human Values. The first lady, on behalf of the president, received Gurudev at the palace and extended her full-hearted support for Art of Living activities in Costa Rica.

Gurudev was fascinated by the orange fire spewing down the side of the volcano as we drove through the rainforest at midnight.

17. SOFTNESS AND FORCEFULNESS

APRIL 15, 1998
EUROPEAN ASHRAM, BAD ANTOGAST, GERMANY

Often people are soft, and their softness comes from lack of courage and forcefulness. They suffer a lot, and at some time or other, they become volatile.

Other people possess a different kind of softness, one that comes from maturity, magnanimity, and knowledge of the Self.

Similarly, there are also two types of forcefulness in people: aggressive and assertive.

Aggressive people are forceful out of weakness or out of fear and insecurity. Assertive people are forceful out of care, love, and compassion.

So, look into yourself and become aware of what type of softness and forcefulness you have.

NEWS FLASH:

Bulgaria, Namibia, and the Dominican Republic joined the Art of Living map this month.

18. THE GOLDEN VEIL

JULY 2, 1997

MONTREAL ASHRAM, CANADA

Craving comes from encouraging the thought of pleasure. Whether you encourage a worldly thought or a Divine thought, they both bring you pleasure.

Worldly thoughts lead you from pleasure down to indulgence, disappointment, and dejection.

Divine thoughts take you from pleasure up to bliss, intelligence, and commitment to service.

Question: What is a Divine thought?

Gurudev: "I am not the body; I am joy; I am unbounded space; I am love; I am peace; I am light."

Question: What is a worldly thought?

Gurudev: It is a thought about money, sex, food, power, status, and self-image.

A worldly thought brings pleasure as memory, yet the actual experience of that pleasure may not be as great as the memory. A Divine thought transforms consciousness.

Truth is hidden by the golden veil of the world. Pierce through this glittering sheath, and know you are the sun.

In the world, many are after GOLD; some are after GOOD; only a few are after GOD.

Transcend GOLD, transcend the GOOD, and reach GOD.

NEWS FLASH:

As silent retreat participants at the Canadian ashram move from the small mind to the Big Mind, the children move super-sized frogs from the small pond to the big lake. Both frogs and humans are happy in their spacious abodes. The new youth course is a big hit with the young people.

19. EXPRESSION AND IMPRESSION

APRIL 2, 1998

KOLKATA, INDIA

Making an effort to express yourself is futile. Effort itself is the biggest impediment to your natural expression. When you don't try, expression comes naturally.

And when you function from your center, your expression is perfect, and you leave a long-lasting impact.

Often you don't seem to have control over your expressions—or the impressions you take in. Wisdom is selecting your expressions and impressions.

Enlightenment is when impressions don't stay at all, whether good or bad. Nature has built a system in us that releases impressions through dreams and through meditation.

Too many impressions in the mind cause:

- Confusion

- Distraction

- Chaos

- Prejudice

- Lack of focus

- Derangement of the mind

Excessive expression makes you lose your depth, your luster, and the serenity of the Self.

Meditation erases the impressions and gives you mastery of your expressions.

20. STUCK IN FEELINGS? ACT

You can transcend feelings when you see that there's something much more fundamental to life than feelings. That something is the Self, which isn't changing at all.

Often instead of concentrating on what you have to do, you sit and ponder over what's happening—both within you and around you. You put so much attention on what's happening rather than on what you're doing.

Do you take responsibility for your feelings, or do you feel helpless about them? The crux of the matter lies there. Why do you give so much importance to your feelings? Your feelings change all the time. You feel good one minute, and the next minute you may feel bad about the same thing. If you feel bad about a particular thing, a little later you feel good about it. When that's the case with your mind, then why anchor your whole life on your feelings, which are so fleeting? They come and go. Just stand up to them. You have to take a leap and go beyond your feelings.

Put attention on what you're doing and leave whatever's happening to Nature. And Nature will carry you through whatever's happening.

Worrying doesn't make any difference, but working does. And spirituality gives one the strength to work.

Put your feelings aside, listen to your intellect, and look at what you need to do. That's it. Know that whatever you have to get, you'll get. Whatever is due to you will come to you. And whatever you need to do, just do it.

21. BEYOND YOUR IDENTITY

The world today faces a crisis. It's fundamentally one of identification. People identify themselves with limited characteristics such as a particular gender, race, religion, region, and nationality, forgetting their basic identity as part of the universal spirit. These limited identifications lead to conflicts: globally and on a personal level.

Every individual is much more than the sum of these limited identifications. The highest identification we can have is that we're part of Divinity. Then comes the identity that we're human beings and members of the one human family.

Let your mind reflect your true nature—you are beauty, you are truth, you are compassion, you are love. See that you are much more than your limited identities or the roles you play—a husband or a wife, a dentist, or a businessperson. You're a beautiful human being on the planet.

We must learn to connect with the entire creation. We must see ourselves through the eyes of quantum physics, viewing the entire universe as a field of energy. Then a big shift happens with your own identity. That is the way to be free.

22. SKEPTICISM

NOVEMBER 1, 1995

LONDON, UNITED KINGDOM

Ignorance is being a skeptic and not knowing it.

A skeptic is stuck in a paradigm that closes off all other possibilities. But this creation contains all possibilities. As you understand how paradigms shift, skepticism drops.

A real scientist can never afford to be a skeptic because skepticism will not probe into unknown areas of existence. Skepticism is an "I know it all" attitude, and this attitude is unscientific. Skepticism is dispelled by knowledge.

Do not recognize someone's skepticism and try to argue. Arguments only strengthen skepticism. Fear of losing one's freedom brings more resistance and causes more skepticism.

Deep inside every human being, there is faith and love—skepticism is only a thin layer. If you hold in your mind, "This person is a skeptic," you only confirm their skepticism.

Your silence and the smile from your heart will dispel any skepticism. There is nothing better than silence to break skepticism. Silence means a quality of consciousness, not just keeping your lips tight.

Skepticism happens only in people who walk with a limited worldview. Children have no skepticism. They live in their fantasy worlds of many possibilities. Their worlds are of innocence, joy, beauty, and love.

23. TENDENCIES AND INFLUENCES

JUNE 20, 2001

STOCKHOLM, SWEDEN

Life is shaped by dual factors: inner tendencies and outer influences. This is what's called *karma*.

Inner tendencies form your attitudes and behavior, while external influences make strong impressions in your mind. Often your tendencies generate external situations, and situations around you can form tendencies within you.

Both—the tendencies from within and the influences from outside—can be either beneficial or harmful.

It's awareness that filters the outer negative influences, and it's awareness that corrects and annihilates the unhealthy inner tendencies. This awareness is called *gyana*, or wisdom. The purpose of education is to develop this awareness so that you can be selective about your tendencies and influences.

It's practically impossible to resist external influences and inner tendencies without raising one's consciousness. This can be gradual or sudden.

When you have a say about your tendencies and your influences, you're free. Only awareness and impeccable devotion can bring this freedom.

NEWS FLASH:

Gurudev's address to the Protestant Christian congregation in Germany was well received. Denmark, Sweden, and Norway had high-energy satsangs. He is moving on to a silent retreat in Gothenburg.

24. DREAMING THE IMPOSSIBLE

DECEMBER 7, 2001

NEW DELHI, INDIA

> *Question*: Gurudev, how can we control daydreams?
>
> *Gurudev*: Dream in the night! (*Laughter*)

What is daydreaming? You have a desire, but you don't have the faith that you can achieve your desire—that's what you call daydreaming.

You can control daydreaming by having a strong goal and believing in it. Like the scientist who wanted to go to the moon and kept dreaming about it—for him, it was the goal of his life, but for others, it was daydreaming.

Either you drop the idea that it will happen, or you believe it will! When you don't know yourself, your potentiality, you have no faith or confidence in your dreams. Once you have faith and confidence in your dreams, they're no longer daydreams!

NEWS FLASH:

Youth volunteers are leading workshops, tree-planting drives, and campaigns for "creating awareness through cleanliness" in rural regions of India. They are also busy transforming villages that have been targeted by militant separatist groups into "model villages." Within a year, three thousand villages in India have been impacted, and five hundred volunteers have been trained.

25. ATTACHMENTS

APRIL 3, 1996
SYDNEY, AUSTRALIA

Being overly attached causes feverish, agitated breath, and feverish breath takes away your peace of mind.

Unfortunately, most people don't notice this until it's too late. Before you get scattered too much or fall prey to misery, gather yourself and rid your breath of the feverishness through surrender (letting go) and *sadhana* (spiritual practices).

When someone is drowning in the ocean of attachments, surrender is the life jacket they can put on and wait to be rescued. Without fighting the attachments, observe the feverish breath and go to the cool place of silence within.

Your first step in this process is to direct your attachment to knowledge, to the Divine.

> *Your nonattachment to the world is your charm.*
> *Your attachment to the Divine is your beauty.*

NEWS FLASH:

At the Chennai satsang, many dignitaries came, including the former president of India and his family.

Then, in Australia, two religious fundamentalists verbally attacked Gurudev as soon as he entered the hall, shocking the audience. Unshaken, Gurudev delivered a powerful and compassionate talk.

Gurudev was sitting in the airport in Perth, Western Australia, when he asked the woman next to him what she did for a living.

"I'm an interior decorator," she said.

"Oh, we do the same job," he replied.

26. WHEN WE ARE JOYFUL

JUNE 19, 1996
SOMEWHERE IN BRITISH COLUMBIA, CANADA

When we're joyful, we don't look for perfection. If you're looking for perfection, then you aren't at the source of joy.

On the surface, the world appears imperfect, but underneath it's all perfect.

> *Perfection hides.*
> *Imperfection shows off.*

The wise won't dwell on the surface but will probe into the depth.

Things aren't blurred; your vision is blurred. An infinite number of actions happen in the wholeness of consciousness, and yet consciousness remains perfect and untouched. As seekers of truth, realize this now and be at home, comfortable, and at ease.

NEWS FLASH:

In Vancouver, representatives of the local indigenous people warmly hosted Gurudev at the University of British Columbia.

There were many reported healings recently. In St. Louis, a man presented a dozen red roses to Gurudev while tears of gratitude rolled down everyone's cheeks. His wife retells the story:

In all our twenty-four years of marriage, my husband Mike has never been one to complain about physical aches and pains. He will go to work no matter how ill he is. I've seen him endure pulled muscles, fever, flu, chronic arthritis, and an abscessed tooth without taking pain medication. So, when he began complaining about his shoulder, I knew it was serious.

A trip to our family doctor resulted in an appointment with a neurologist. The MRI showed damage to nerves and muscles; the diagnosis after X-rays was a torn rotator cuff. Surgery was scheduled for June 13 at 10:00 a.m.

When we received a flyer in the mail about a lecture and meditation with Gurudev Sri Sri Ravi Shankar, scheduled for June 12, we thought it would be a good way to spend the evening just before the surgery.

Many of the things we heard during the talk sounded familiar. Gurudev's voice even sounded familiar! We felt a real need to speak to Gurudev, and despite a line that seemed to be three hundred people long, we took our place. Mike is usually not too patient, and since he was in pain, I still can't explain why we stood there to meet someone we would probably never see again.

And what do you say to a holy man you know nothing about? "Nice to meet you?" "How are you?" With so many people, would he even care about two more?

After saying hello, I found myself asking him for my husband's safety during the next day's surgery. Embarrassed by making such a request to a complete stranger, I returned to my seat.

Gurudev turned to someone behind him and asked for a rose. He handed it to Mike and said to keep the rose by his side during the night and "all will be well."

On the way home, we discussed the whole evening and decided that the rose was a "sweet gesture" and that Gurudev was a "nice man." How our perception would grow over the next few days!

The next day Mike checked into the hospital. Our doctor said the routine surgery would take about an hour. Twenty minutes later, I looked up and saw the doctor motioning for me. He had such an odd look on his face. I asked if he had just killed Mike, since not enough time had elapsed to complete the procedure.

He shook his head and said, "I can't explain what happened. When we cut into Mike's shoulder, there was no tear. I checked the MRI twice. It's on the MRI, but he doesn't have it now. My assistant is closing now."

The next morning it dawned on us that the holy man must have healed Mike's shoulder! We called the Art of Living Center in St. Louis to find out where Gurudev was staying. We got directions and off we went.

When we arrived, kind people helped me to get Mike settled in a chair while we waited for Gurudev, whose presence I felt even before he entered the room. Thankfully, Mike was able to tell his story, as I was too overwhelmed to speak.

Gurudev asked only two questions of my husband: "All is well?" and, after Mike's story, "What is an MRI?"

Someone explained an MRI, and Gurudev's response was, "Oh, there is a machine that makes a picture of what I can see?"

—Cathy Champion

27. THE PRIMAL INSTINCT

APRIL 10, 1997

RISHIKESH, INDIA

Fear comes from an impression of the past. We experience the fear in the present moment and project it on the future. When people deny fear, they become stiff and unnatural; when they recognize and accept fear, they go beyond it and become free.

Total lack of fear is possible only in utter chaos or utmost orderliness.

Neither a fool nor a saint has fear. But for everyone in between, there's fear.

Fear is a primal instinct, essential to preserve orderliness in the world.

Fear of death preserves life. Fear of sickness brings hygiene. Fear of doing wrong, and the misery it brings, keeps you righteous.

A pinch of fear is necessary to keep things moving smoothly. A child has a pinch of fear, so it is careful and alert while walking.

Fear is love standing upside down and can be totally transformed through the awareness of Divine love.

28. DEDICATION AND COMMITMENT

MAY 21, 1997

VIENNA, AUSTRIA

Your car runs out of fuel, and you have to refill it again and again.

In the same way, your dedication and commitment run out over time and need constant renewal! You have to dedicate and rededicate, again and again.

Often people take their dedication for granted—and the mind starts to demand or complain. When your dedication isn't full, it leads to grumbling and complaints.

Total dedication brings enormous enthusiasm, zeal, and trust and doesn't leave any room for small-mindedness.

29. INTELLECT

DECEMBER 3, 1997

CALICUT, INDIA

Debates, discussions, and contemplation nourish the intellect. Prejudice, stigmas, and dogmas are detrimental to the intellect.

The intellect harbors inhibitions, likes and dislikes, approvals and disapprovals. The intellect also harbors wisdom, which brings forth intuition.

Question: Is intuition beyond intellect?

Gurudev: Yes, but it shines through the intellect.

Question: Are emotions and intellect contradictory?

Gurudev: They can be contradictory.

Question: When there's a conflict between emotions and intellect, which is better?

Gurudev: Pure intellect rises beyond conflicts—it's not caught up in the emotional turbulence of the mind.

Usually, the intellect gets colored by emotions and becomes impure, like muddy water. Then it's unable to reflect the Self. A pure intellect, still and serene, reflects the Self.

Question: Is intellect affected by one's *karma*?

Gurudev: *Karma* doesn't afflict the pure intellect.

Liberation, enlightenment purifies the intellect. The Sanskrit word for intellect is *buddhi*; one who is liberated is a *buddha*; one with little intelligence is *buddhu* (foolish).

30. A WISE PERSON IS HAPPY EVEN IN BAD TIMES

NEW YEAR'S EVE, 1997

GERMAN ACADEMY

People who serve will have good times even in bad times.

When there is famine or war, Red Cross workers will be fine because they're serving. The more relief they can bring to others, the happier they feel.

On the other hand, selfish people who live just for their own enjoyment will be miserable, even in good times.

In good times, people often lose their happiness over a small thing. Hosts often do not enjoy their parties because some little thing is missing; they forgot to invite somebody, somebody did not come, or some little thing went wrong. A wise person is happy even in bad times. A foolish person is unhappy even in good times.

You make time good or bad. People usually blame the bad times and wait for the good times. But even if an astrologer says you're in a hopeless time, you can make it good!

> *Like the weather, time has its own impact on you. Doing your spiritual practices and going to satsangs are your shield, your protection.*

Realize that you're more than time and that you can move through time with your timeless connection to the Divine. Don't feel shy to speak about human and spiritual values; the time has come to share those with the whole world!

31. FOCUS AND EXPANSION

NOVEMBER 26, 1998
BANGALORE ASHRAM, INDIA

Focus sharpens the mind, and relaxation expands the mind. An expanded mind without sharpness can't bring holistic development. At the same time, a sharp mind without expansion causes tension, anger, and frustration.

The balance between the focused mind and an expanded consciousness brings perfection.

SKY Breath Meditation and the silent retreat techniques are aimed at developing a consciousness that's both sharp and unbounded.

Service and commitment play a major role in this. Food and attitude also have an effect.

Expanded consciousness is peace and joy. Focused consciousness is love and creativity.

Just as the magnifying glass both focuses the sun and can also expand the letters on a page, our consciousness gives us a bigger vision *and* sharper focus.

The individual self is a point of focused consciousness. When every atom of the expanded consciousness becomes sharp, focused, that is the awakening of Divinity in you.

32. FAITH—A QUALITY OF UNDIVIDED CONSCIOUSNESS

MAY 27, 1999

EUROPEAN ASHRAM, BAD ANTOGAST, GERMANY

Don't make that which you have faith in an object of knowing. The moment you make something an object of knowing, analysis starts, and doubt follows.

You have faith in God; don't try to know God. You have faith in the Self; don't try to know the Self. God and Self aren't objects of knowing. You can't have faith in that which you make an object of knowing.

A child has faith in the mother and does not make her into an object of knowing. The child does not try to know the mother; the child simply has faith in her. You can't make love an object of knowing—if you try to know it, it'll disappear. When you have faith in something, what is the need to know it?

In the same way, God, love, sleep, and Self are all beyond knowing.

Faith is synthesis; knowing is analysis.

Analysis creates a distance; synthesis brings it together.

Faith is the nature of an undivided mind, an undivided consciousness.

Question: Can you have faith without being aware of it?

Gurudev: Yes. Faith is simply a relaxed, stable quality of consciousness.

NEWS FLASH:

Seva camps are in full swing in Bangalore with a particular focus on differently abled and gifted children. Seva camps are also held in other areas.

33. NEGATIVITY NEEDS AN ANCHOR

SEPTEMBER 9, 1999

BANGALORE ASHRAM, INDIA

> *Negativity can't remain without support.*
> *Positivity and happiness can exist without any reason.*

The mind goes on trying to find support for its negativity. It looks for a hook to hang its negativity—if not this person, then that thing or that person—this perpetuates *maya* (delusion).

The creeping vine of negativity needs support in order to grow. But negativity or aversion for even one person can make you miserable—you don't need anything else!

All negativity is an indicator for you to move to your center and broaden your vision to cosmic intelligence. So instead of focusing your attention on support for your negativity, look to the seed of negativity.

SKY breathing, meditation, and silence help you transcend negativity.

34. ADORATION

NOVEMBER 15, 2001

BANGALORE ASHRAM, INDIA

Adoration shows the magnanimity of the one who adores, rather than the one who is adored! Adoration is an indicator that the ego has become transparent. The best antidote for ego is adoration.

Adoration works in three ways:

- If it's for someone else, it's not palatable to an egotistic person.

- If it's for you, it boosts your ego.

- If it's you adoring someone else, it dissolves your ego and makes you big-hearted and kind.

A person with low self-esteem cringes when adored. And the arrogant ones can't tolerate others being adored.

- A desire for adoration is a sign of immaturity.

- Aversion to adoration is small-mindedness.

- Lack of adoration in life is dryness and boredom.

- A healthy mind always likes to adore, to elevate others.

- An unhealthy mind likes to pull everything down. Adoration indicates the trust, enthusiasm, and richness in a culture.

- Lack of adoration indicates a self-centered, small-minded, fearful, and culturally impoverished society.

Adoration doesn't sway one who's great. The test of a person's greatness is that one is unshaken by any amount of adoration. Being indifferent to adoration when it comes to you and being generous when it's to be given is the way of the wise!

35. *MAYA*

DECEMBER 21, 2001

BANGALORE ASHRAM, INDIA

What is *maya* (delusion or non-Reality)?

Maya is that which can be measured. The whole world can be measured; that's why it's *maya*. All five elements—earth, water, fire, air, and space—can be measured.

Measurement is always relative and not absolute. For example, if something weighs six kilograms on Earth, it will weigh only one kilogram on the moon.

All measurements only provide a relative understanding. Einstein's theory of relativity—that measurements of space and time differ according to the motion of the observer—correlates with the *advaita* (non-dual) philosophy, which says that everything that is perceived through the senses is *maya*.

The light of the star you see today is not really today's light. It can take years for the light to reach you! Both size and weight change in air, water, and earth. So "measure" is illusive and not dependable. Your bones, skin, body, environment, and the five elements can be measured; you can put a value, a quantity, to them. So the whole world is *maya*!

So what is not *maya*? All that can't be measured. You can't say one ounce of love, two ounces of peace, and five kilograms of happiness. Can *you* be measured? It's not possible. Your body has weight, but not *you*.

Truth can't be measured, joy can't be measured, and beauty can't be measured. All these are part of consciousness or the Divine and aren't *maya*.

36. THE IMPERMANENCE OF *MAYA*

Maya also means that which is always changing. The ever-changing events and things around you are what *maya* is. When someone says, "You are drowned in *maya*," it means you are drowned in small little things that aren't permanent. When you're "logged on" to the ever-changing *maya*, life is very unstable. Stability comes when you log on to something in you that's not changing, which remains the same throughout time. That's called "*getting out of the web of* maya."

There is still another meaning of *maya*—that which has an appearance, but when you try to catch it, it doesn't get into your hand. That is how everything in the world is. You see something so beautiful, and you try to possess it. The moment you possess it, you find the beauty is gone. It's no longer where you thought it was. You think happiness is out there and you chase after that; when you get there, it's not there.

If you are stable, still, and content within yourself, then everything runs toward you.

37. CREATIVITY

AUGUST 6, 2002
EUROPEAN ASHRAM, BAD ANTOGAST, GERMANY

Creativity brings a new beginning for "time." When you're creative, you break the monotony of time. Everything becomes fresh and alive. Creativity brings along with it a new round of enthusiasm. Both creative and procreative impulses in nature are associated with enthusiasm. When you're enthusiastic, you're closer to the creative principle of existence.

Deep silence is the mother of creativity. No creativity can come out of one who's too busy, worried, over-ambitious, or lethargic. Balanced activity, rest, and yoga can kindle skills and creativity in you.

NEWS FLASH:

The chief of twelve million Native Americans signed a Memorandum of Understanding with Gurudev in a moving ceremony, in which Gurudev was formally invited to the United States and requested to work in close cooperation for the betterment of the Indigenous people.

38. THE DIFFERENT KINDS OF UNDERSTANDING

OCTOBER 14, 1998

MONTREAL ASHRAM, CANADA

There are three kinds of understanding: intellectual understanding, experiential understanding, and existential realization.

Intellectual understanding says "yes"; it agrees. Experiential understanding feels "it is obvious." Existential realization is irrefutable. It becomes your very nature.

All you hear will simply remain a jumble of words if there's no experiential understanding, which is more on the feeling level. You can know intellectually that your deepest nature is peace and joy, but sitting and feeling that you're peaceful and joyful is totally different.

When one gets an experience, one wants to understand more about it and becomes a seeker. If you have only intellectual understanding, you'll think you know it all. Most theologians are in this category.

Existential realization combines experiential and intellectual understanding. But it's beyond both of these.

> *Question*: How do we get there?
>
> *Gurudev*: There is no way. When the fruit becomes ripe, it falls.
>
> *Question*: What is doubt?
>
> *Gurudev*: It is one part of the mind challenging the other part of the mind.

Meditation

1. MEDITATION IS ABSOLUTE COMFORT

Meditation is the journey from movement to stillness, from sound to silence.

The need to meditate is present in every human being because it's a natural tendency of human life to look for a joy that doesn't diminish and for a love that doesn't distort or turn into negative emotions.

Is meditation foreign to you? Absolutely not. You were in meditation for a couple of months before your birth, in your mother's womb, doing nothing. You didn't even have to chew your food—it was fed directly into your belly, and you were there happily floating in the fluid, turning and kicking, sometimes here and sometimes there, but most of the time happily floating. That is meditation or absolute comfort. You did nothing; everything was done for you.

So there's a natural tendency in every human being, in every soul, to crave that state of absolute comfort. And getting back to that state you have tasted—just before entering the hustle-bustle of this world—is very natural because, in this universe, everything is cyclic. Everything wants to go back to its source, just as the leaves let go and return to the soil in fall.

The natural tendency to recycle all that we have collected in day-to-day life as impressions, get rid of them, and get back to the original state we were in when we came to this planet is what meditation is. Becoming fresh and alive again is what meditation is. Getting back to that serenity that is your original nature is meditation.

2. KICK THE BALL AND BE IN THE GOAL

JANUARY 4, 2001

MONTREAL ASHRAM, CANADA

Do you know why the earth is shaped like a ball?

(Silence . . .)

So you can kick it, and it will roll away!

From the moment you wake up in the morning, you're with people, and your mind is caught up in worldly thoughts. So, sometime during the day, sit for a few minutes with your eyes closed, get into the cave of your heart, and kick the world away like a ball.

But as soon as you open your eyes, hold on to the ball because you need to kick it again in the next session. (*Laughter*)

During the day, be 100 percent attached to the work; don't try to detach yourself. But when you sit for meditation, then totally detach yourself. Only those who can totally detach can take total responsibility.

Eventually you'll be able to be both attached and detached simultaneously. Kick the ball and be in the goal! This is the skill of living—the *art of living*.

3. YOUR NATURE IS PEACE

MARCH 16, 2002

RISHIKESH, INDIA

Peace is your nature, yet you remain restless. Freedom is your nature, yet you remain in bondage. Happiness is your nature, yet you become miserable for some reason or another. Contentment is your nature, yet you continue to reel in desires. Benevolence is your nature, yet you do not reach out.

Spiritual practice is going toward your nature. It's becoming what you truly are. Your true nature is peace, infinity, beauty—the Self.

4. THREE GOLDEN PRINCIPLES FOR MEDITATION

There are three golden principles for meditation.

The first is "I want nothing." Not even a glass of water. I'm not expecting you to want nothing in your life. If you want many things, just keep them aside for now. For the next few minutes, "I want nothing."

When you want nothing, you also do nothing.

The second golden rule is "I do nothing." Can you just be, doing nothing? I'm not going to be mindful. If the mind drifts somewhere, let it drift. You only breathe. Do not make an effort to think either "I want nothing" or "I do nothing." It is just an effortless attention before meditation.

The third step is "I am nothing." You have to let go of all the labels you put on yourself, including being a teacher, a businessperson, a man or a woman, a scholar or whatever. You let go of all these labels and say, "I am nothing." Also, if you think you're very wise, forget it. If you think you're stupid, you're in the same boat. If you think you're too poor or too rich, there's no way you'll be able to meditate. If you think you're very holy or a sinner, that you're somebody great or worthless, then also you can't settle down into the deepest core of your being. After meditation, you can again be something. It's your choice.

I want nothing. I do nothing. I am nothing.

These three basic principles let your mind be free from the outer stimuli with which it engages, day in and day out. The mind goes to its source and there it becomes no-mind. To settle into the consciousness of which all of us are made up, this must be our initial step. It is the journey from sound to silence.

5. ADVICE FROM HAWAII

JANUARY 24, 1996
KAUA'I, HAWAII, UNITED STATES

What type of time do you give to prayer and meditation?

Usually you give it leftover time, when no guests are coming, there are no nice movies to watch, no parties or weddings to attend, no shopping to do, no social media posts to read. This is not quality time.

If your prayers aren't answered, it's because you've never given them quality time. Give satsang and meditation your highest priority.

Give prime time to the Divine. You'll be rewarded.

NEWS FLASH:

Riddle: *What is most freely given, yet not taken?*

1. Compliments? (. . . No.)

2. Blame? (. . . No, people take blame.)

3. Money? (. . . No, money is readily taken, not freely given.)

4. Happiness? (. . . Nobody can give happiness.)

5. ??

Clue: It hangs in space like an orphan. No one owns it. Like an overripe papaya in Hawaii, it rots. The answer to this riddle lies in the title. ALOHA!

6. DEEP REST AND BLISS

JUNE 7, 2001

BERLIN, GERMANY

Deep rest is bliss.

Bliss is the understanding that only God exists.

This conviction or experience that "only God exists" is the deepest rest possible—*samadhi*.

Samadhi is the mother of all talents, strengths, and virtues. *Samadhi* is needed even for the most materialistic person because a materialistic person looks to gain strength and virtues. To be in *samadhi*, you don't need any effort or talents, strengths, or virtues.

Withdrawing from all types of physical and mental activity is rest. That's built into our system as sleep, and sleep is the best friend of activity.

Samadhi is conscious rest. It's the best friend of life. To be alive in your full potential, *samadhi* is indispensable.

What obstructs *samadhi* is restlessness. How many types of restlessness are there, and what are the remedies? (For the answer, read the next note.)

NEWS FLASH:

The Art of Living course has now been held in 132 countries. Last week, the course was held in Jordan.

7. FIVE TYPES OF RESTLESSNESS

JUNE 14, 2001
EUROPEAN ASHRAM, BAD ANTOGAST, GERMANY

There are five types of restlessness.

The first type of restlessness is due to the place you are in. When you move away from that place—the street or the house—you immediately feel better. Singing, being with children playing, and laughing can change this atmospheric restlessness. When you sing, the vibration in the place changes.

The second type of restlessness is in the body. Eating the wrong food or *vata-aggravating* food,[3] eating at odd times, not exercising, and overworking can all cause physical restlessness. The remedy for this is exercise, moderation in work habits, and going on a vegetable or juice diet for one or two days.

The third type of restlessness is mental restlessness. It is caused by ambition, strong thoughts, likes or dislikes. Knowledge alone can cure this restlessness: seeing life from a broader perspective, knowing the Self, and realizing the impermanence of everything. If you achieve everything, so what? After your achievement, you will die. Knowledge of your mortality, confidence in the Self, in the Divine, can all calm down this mental restlessness.

Then there is emotional restlessness—when you feel empty, lonely, or meaningless. Any amount of knowledge does not help here. Only SKY Breath Meditation helps. All the emotional restlessness vanishes after practicing SKY. Singing and dancing also helps. The presence of your spiritual teacher, a wise person, or a saint will also help to calm your emotional restlessness.

The fifth type of restlessness is rare. It is the restlessness of the soul. When everything feels empty and meaningless, know you are very fortunate. That longing and restlessness is the restlessness of the soul. Don't try to get rid of it. Embrace it! Welcome it! Usually to get rid of it, people do all sorts of things—change locations, jobs, or partners. They do this, do that. It seems to help for some time, but it doesn't really.

This restlessness of the soul alone can bring authentic prayer in you. It brings perfection and miracles in life. It is so precious to get this innermost longing for the Divine. Satsang and the presence of an enlightened one soothe the restlessness of the soul.

---

3   According to Ayurveda, the ancient Vedic system of health, vata-aggravating food increases the element of air and space in the body—often causing indigestion and pain.

After a memorable satsang in the biggest cathedral in Berlin, Gurudev moved on to London. Westminster Abbey and Brent Town Hall hosted satsangs, and Gurudev inaugurated our new Art of Living Center in London.

On the thirteenth, he arrived in Strasbourg to deliver a talk at the European Parliament. It was presided over by Reinhold Messner, the famous Italian mountaineer, and Peter von Kohl, the president of the Organization of Journalists of the European Parliament.

8. THE FIVE STEPS IN MEDITATION

JULY 2, 2002

WASHINGTON, D.C., UNITED STATES

We spend so much time keeping the body safe and making it comfortable. The mind gets stuck in the perishable body.

Can you preserve this body forever? One day it will surely drop away.

Before the body drops you, learn to drop the body. The body dropping you is death, and you dropping the body is meditation. Ultimately, the mind will become one with the spirit and the body with the earth.

In the beginning, meditation brings relaxation. In the second step, meditation gives you energy. In the third step, meditation brings forth creativity. In the fourth step, meditation creates enthusiasm and joy. The fifth step of meditation is indescribable. You feel oneness with the whole universe.

Don't stop before reaching the fifth step.

Don't stop with just some relaxation, some joy, enthusiasm, or the fulfillment of desires. Your ability to enjoy and fulfill your desires increases with meditation.

When you don't want anything for yourself, you're able to fulfill the desires of others as well.

Gurudev went to Heidelberg and Berlin in Germany, where people came in large numbers to attend talks and satsangs. While there, he was received at the Indian embassy and met with several senators from the German parliament.

9. MEDITATION: FOOD FOR THE SOUL

Meditation is food for the soul. When you're hungry, spontaneously you go to eat something. If you're thirsty, you want to drink some water. In the same way, the soul yearns for meditation and this tendency is in everyone.

The problem is that we try to look for that satisfaction where it isn't available. It's like going to a grocery store when you want to put gas in your car. So the right direction needs to be found.

Meditation is uplifting the energy and mind and spreading it out. There is something in you that expands when you're happy and contracts when you're unhappy. But we never pay attention to what's contracting and expanding on the inside—we only focus on the outside. We don't pay attention to the reason.

Even a glimpse of this consciousness, this energy inside you, can make the smile on your face so strong that nothing whatsoever can take it away from you. Life assumes another dimension suddenly. You don't have to abandon everything. Just being amid all the noise and still recognizing that beauty, that thing that's so beautiful, so wonderful, so fascinating, right here and now, is meditation.

10. GETTING STEEPED IN MYSTERY IS DEVOTION

OCTOBER 7, 2000

BANGALORE ASHRAM, INDIA

If you're not amazed by the magnificence of this creation, your eyes are not yet opened. Once your eyes are opened, they close, and this is meditation. (*Laughter*)

Tell me, what is *not* a mystery in this creation? Birth is a mystery; death is a mystery. And life is certainly a greater mystery, isn't it?

Being completely immersed in the mystery of life and this creation is *samadhi* (that experience of very deep rest and a sense of total peace within yourself).

Your knowing or believing doesn't really matter to what *is*.

This creation is an unfathomable secret, and its mysteries only deepen.

The "scene"—what you see—is a mystery; the "seer"—the person seeing—is a mystery.

Deepening the mystery of creation is science. Deepening the mystery of the Self is spirituality.

They're two sides of the same coin. If neither science nor spirituality can create wonder and devotion in you, then you're in deep slumber.

NEWS FLASH:

Every day during the Navratri celebration, poor people were fed at the Bangalore Ashram. More than five thousand people in the slums were given clothes. Gurudev has just emerged from his weeklong silence looking radiant. News about healing experiences continues to flood in from all over the world.

11. IF YOU CANNOT MEDITATE—TRY THIS!

JUNE 17, 1998

BALTIMORE, MARYLAND, UNITED STATES

If you're unable to meditate, if your mind is chattering too much and nothing works, just feel that you're a little stupid. Then you'll be able to sink deep into your practice.

> *Your intellect is a tiny part of your total consciousness. If you're stuck in the intellect, you miss out on a lot.*
>
> *Happiness is when you transcend the intellect. When you feel stupid or in deep love or awe, you transcend the intellect.*

Question: How do you go beyond the intellect?

Gurudev: By acting stupid! Everyone avoids being stupid; no one wants to look dumb. *That* is really stupid.

Stupidity should be followed by meditation; otherwise depression may follow.

NEWS FLASH:

Gurudev attended the Baltimore conference on Breaking the Cycle of Violence. The Art of Living prison program team gave presentations on the health benefits of SKY Breath Meditation and the prison program—including the women's program and groundbreaking independent research on juvenile offenders. The Art of Living panel stirred up a storm of interest with the enthusiastic audience.

12. THE GREAT PLEASURE OF REST

JULY 19, 2001

MONTREAL ASHRAM, CANADA

There's pleasure in rest and pleasure in activity. The pleasure in activity is momentary and causes fatigue, while the pleasure in rest is enduring and energizing. So to the one who has tasted pleasure in rest (*samadhi*), the pleasure in activity is insignificant. The real pleasure is in *samadhi*.

Activity is part of the system. In order to have deep rest, one must be active. The proper balance of both is essential. In fact, it's only in wisdom that deep rest happens.

13. DROP YOUR INTENTIONS

OCTOBER 29, 2001

BANGALORE ASHRAM, INDIA

A strong tendency to keep doing something, whether important or unimportant, becomes an impediment to meditation.

"Doing" starts first with an intention and then translates into action. Though intention springs from being, when it becomes a "doing," it doesn't let you settle down. All intentions, good or bad, trivial or important, need to be dropped for meditation to happen.

> *Question*: But isn't dropping all intentions itself an intention?
>
> *Gurudev*: Yes, but this intention is the last and necessary one. Dropping intentions isn't an act. Just the intention to drop the intentions itself serves the purpose. Dropping all intentions, even for a moment, brings you in touch with your Self, and in that instant, meditation happens.

While you sit for meditation, you have to let the world be the way it is. The repetition of meditation is to habituate your system to stop and start activity at will. The ability to consciously do this is a precious skill.

14. NO REACTION, JUST OBSERVATION

Apart from meditation, every day make a little time, even three to ten minutes, to just be still and observe the nature around you. We experience stillness when we meditate. But with eyes open, we can also experience stillness. When we make a habit of experiencing stillness, it also helps a great deal in your activity.

Fix your gaze, sit still, and observe what is happening in the body and the environment. When we're active all the time, our capacity to observe goes down. Even while looking at beautiful scenery—a blooming flower, a tranquil lake—if the mind is constantly chattering, you lose the whole joy of the moment. Just let the river flow and let nature be *as it is*, rather than labeling it and thinking about it in the mind.

When you drop the internal dialogue, then you enjoy.

This becomes possible by doing this short practice time and again. You can absorb all that's happening without the chatter in the mind. And only you can stop the chatter.

There are many ways. A big shock can stop the chatter in the mind. Or if you consciously say, "I am just going to be here, now, and observe what is," that also can stop the mind's chatter. A few minutes of such exercise can bring an inner strength that will help you to drop the reactive tendency, which has become habitual in life.

No reaction, just observation.

15. MEDITATION: GOING DEEPER INTO THE "I"

The way to know yourself is just knowing you are the experiencer, not the experiences.

We go through many experiences in life, pleasant experiences, unpleasant experiences. We say, "I am experiencing. I am agitated. I am angry. I am upset. I'm sad or I'm happy. I'm peaceful. I'm great. I'm feeling wonderful." But this

"I," is to be seen as different from "I'm this," "I'm that," "I'm all those experiences." Because experiences change, but the "I" doesn't change.

And going deep into this "I" is meditation. Seeing yourself beyond the thoughts, beyond your notions, beyond your concept of what's happening to you or what others are and who you are. Can you step back and say, "I'm not this, I am not this, I am not this, I am nothing"?

Then you come to a very peaceful place within yourself. You'll find you'll feel so connected.

Service: Giving Back and Making a Difference

1. THE PURPOSE OF LIFE

NOVEMBER 12, 1998

BANGALORE ASHRAM, INDIA

Our first and foremost commitment in life is to do service.

If there's fear or confusion in your life, it's because of a lack of commitment.

The very thought *I'm here in this world to do service* dissolves the "I," and when the "I" dissolves, worries dissolve. Service is not something you do out of convenience or for pleasure. The ultimate purpose of life is to be of service.

An uncommitted mind is miserable. A committed mind may experience rough weather but will reap the fruits of its labor.

When you make service your sole purpose in life, it eliminates fear, brings focus, purposefulness, action, long-term joy—and sometimes short-term problems! (*Laughter*) A little discomfort in the short-term for a long-term good.

2. SERVICE SERVES YOU

JUNE 13, 1996

ST. LOUIS, MISSOURI, UNITED STATES

The way to expand from individual to universal consciousness is to share others' sorrows and joys. As you grow, your consciousness should also grow.

When you expand in consciousness over time, depression is not possible. Your innermost source is joy.

The way to overcome personal misery is to share universal misery! The way to expand personal joy is to share universal joy.

Instead of thinking, *What about me?* and *What can I gain from this world?*, think, *What can I do for the world?*

When everyone comes from the place of contributing to society, we'll have an enlightened society. We have to educate ourselves and culture our individual consciousness to expand over time from "What about me?" to "What can I contribute?"

If you're not having deep experiences in meditation, then do more service—you'll gain merit, and your meditation will go deeper. When you bring some relief or freedom to someone through service, good vibrations and blessings come to you.

> *Service brings merit.*
> *Merit allows you to go deeper in meditation.*
> *Meditation brings back your smile.*

NEWS FLASH:

Today marks the end of the first year of the weekly knowledge sheets. The year started in Big Sur and is ending in St. Louis; it began in *knowledge* and is concluding in *service* for others. Weekly knowledge sheets now go to more than three hundred Art of Living satsang groups, touching seven thousand people every week around the world.

After a quick two-day stopover in Boston with overflowing crowds at Interface and Harvard's Kennedy School of Government and with lively late night satsangs, Gurudev arrived in Pittsburgh to a packed schedule of satsangs held in people's homes, temple visits, two lectures, and a celebration to inaugurate our new Art of Living Center.

Afterward, at a private party, Gurudev distributed the celebration cake by tossing the cake-laden plates to the people sitting around him in the room—carrying on his tradition of high-spirited humor and playfulness. Seeing the crumbs and icing "decorating" her usually pristine living room, the hostess managed to maintain only a slightly strained smile. She understood that her teacher spattered her carpet with love to point out her over-attachment (something she was famous for). Had anyone else done this, they would have been in big trouble.

3. SERVICE BLESSINGS

FEBRUARY 19, 1997

MAUI, HAWAII, UNITED STATES

When you do service, don't think you're doing a favor for somebody. Your service has rewarded you immediately. Your reward is certain and is always more than your doing. Your expectation of reward turns service into labor.

If you think you've done a lot, you'll do very little. Just see that you've done little; then you'll do more.

Service means that even when you don't see an immediate reward, there's no complaint.

Labor means that even after an immediate reward, there are complaints.

Be grateful for any opportunity to do service.

4. WHEN TO LET GO AND WHEN TO SERVE

You're bothered by negative emotions and qualities. Dropping all the negativity that you don't want to carry or that you can't handle is letting go. Unless you let go, sorrow will never leave you.

Life is full of opposite values, highs and lows. Keep the mind steady in spite of ups and downs in life. During challenging times, face it, and be with the knowledge that this will also change. During good times, give a channel to your happiness: Have an attitude of service and serve everyone to your best capacity. When you're upset, let go, and when you're happy, serve.

Letting go and being of service—both go together in life. So serve when you're happy and let go when you are miserable.

When you let go of joy, it multiplies. When you let go of sorrow, it dissolves.

Repose in your infinite Being, which is beyond the phenomena happening around you.

5. VOLUNTEER

NOVEMBER 9, 2001
TAIPEI, TAIWAN

Who's a volunteer? One who's self-motivated and inspired, and who will come to help without being asked.

It's possible for a volunteer's motivation to diminish, leading to frustration. When a volunteer's attitude comes from demand rather than humility, it dilutes the quality of their service.

Slipping away from commitment by thinking there's no boss is another pitfall for a volunteer—for example, thinking, *If I like it, I'll do it. If I don't like it, I won't do it!* A car can't move smoothly if the individual wheels refuse to be guided by the steering wheel. The team working on the construction of a building has to accept the authority of the structural engineer, their "boss."

All these problems can only be overcome by being more grounded in spiritual knowledge. A volunteer devoid of a spiritual dimension is utterly weak.

- A volunteer needs to stick to his commitment.
- The integrity of a volunteer comes from his spiritual practices.
- The authority of the project leader needs to be acknowledged by the volunteers working for that project.
- The strength of a volunteer comes from the challenges they're ready and willing to face.
- A volunteer moves beyond his boundaries when he finds he's capable of doing so much more than he ever thought possible.
- A true volunteer doesn't expect appreciation or reward. He's thoroughly mistaken if he thinks he's obliging somebody.
- People volunteer because they derive joy from it. That joy itself is the reward and is immediate. It doesn't come on the first of every month in the form of a salary! When volunteers realize this, they're filled with gratitude.

When volunteers waver from within, their support system is spiritual wisdom and good friends.

NEWS FLASH:

In Delhi, Gurudev addressed the UN Conference on Volunteerism. In Taipei, Taiwan, Gurudev blessed the inauguration of the Museum of World Religions, in the company of the Taiwanese prime minister. The founder of the museum, Zen Master Hsin Tao, came and met with Gurudev last night and expressed his gratitude. Tomorrow, Gurudev will speak on "The Preservation of Sacred Sites."

6. CHRISTMAS MESSAGE: YOUR GIFTS ARE FOR OTHERS

Message for Christmas:

You are the Christmas tree that points upward with branches on all sides. At the time of year when other trees are barren, you are green with many gifts to offer.

You bear gifts and lights—not for yourself, but for others. Remember that all the gifts you are carrying in your life are for others. Anyone who comes to you, offer them your gifts.

The Spiritual Path:
Expanding Your Awareness

1. THE FIRST STEP ON THE SPIRITUAL PATH

The first step on the spiritual path is to stop blaming yourself. People blame themselves saying, "Oh, I did this wrong; I'm no good."

What is a spiritual path? It's going inward to be in touch with yourself at the core of your being. When you blame someone else, do you want to be around them? So, if you blame yourself, how can you go deep within yourself?

The biggest impediment to meditation is self-blame. Self-blame prevents you from settling down. And if you can't settle down, you start to blame others around you.

We oscillate between self-blame and blaming others. We judge ourselves too much or we judge others—either we're not all right or someone else is wrong. Wake up and stop judging. Don't be too hard on yourself.

You're part of a phenomenon that's happening. Like the trees, the rivers, and the birds are here, you're also here. So many birds have taken birth, and so many birds have died. So many trees have sprouted and grown, and they've all vanished. Like this, so many people have come into this world, and they'll all pass on. Then new people will come and go. This planet has been here like this for billions of years.

We don't see that this is how things are. When you see your life from a bigger context, then you stop blaming yourself.

We need to find that fine balance to recognize shortcomings without blame. Not denying and not blaming but recognizing. The mere recognition itself takes you further.

So the first step on the spiritual path is to stop blaming yourself and to stop blaming others. Then you are able to go within yourself. And when you go within yourself, you find there is no other.

The formula of love is this: There is no other.

2. THE ONLY THING YOU MUST REMEMBER

OCTOBER 5, 1995
BANGALORE ASHRAM, INDIA

The only thing you must remember is how fortunate you are. When you forget this, you become sad.

Sorrow indicates your attachment to negative qualities *and* your attachment to positive qualities.

Your negative qualities make you sad, and so do your positive qualities. And when you think you're so great and start blaming others, that also makes you become sad.

When you compare your qualities with others, you become sad.

Sorrow can bring you back to the Self, which is all joy. But this realization is possible only through knowledge—awareness. Without knowledge, sorrow does not seem to end; instead it multiplies. Knowledge completes sorrow.

Only with the power of knowledge, do you transcend sorrow.

On this path you have everything. This beautiful Knowledge is complete with all flavors in it: wisdom, laughter, service, silence, singing, dancing, celebration, sacred ceremonies . . . and complaints, problems, complications, and chaos to add spice.

Life is so colorful!

3. SIX SIGNS OF A SEEKER

OCTOBER 1, 1997
BANGALORE ASHRAM, INDIA

1. Acknowledging that one knows very little.
    Many people think they know without knowing, or they get stuck in their limited knowledge. So they never learn. So the first thing is to acknowledge that one knows very little.

2. Willingness to know.
   Many people acknowledge that they don't know, but they're not ready to learn.

3. Being nonjudgmental and open-minded.
   Some people would like to learn, but their judgmental attitude and close-mindedness don't allow them to learn.

4. Total commitment and one-pointedness to the path one has chosen.
   Some people are open-minded but lack commitment and one-pointedness. They keep shopping here and there and never progress.

5. Always putting truth and service before pleasure.
   Sometimes even committed and one-pointed people stay away from the path in pursuit of momentary pleasures.

6. Patience and perseverance.
   Some people are not swayed by pleasures and are committed and one-pointed, but if they lack patience and perseverance, they become restless and dejected.

4. LETTING GO

OCTOBER 24, 1995
MONTREAL ASHRAM, CANADA

Attaining higher states of consciousness doesn't require any complicated strategy; one just needs to learn to let go.

Usually, we tend to let go of pleasant emotions and hold on to the unpleasant ones. But when your consciousness becomes free and cultured through meditation, this tendency of holding on to one's negative emotions is the first thing to disappear. We start living in the moment.

As your consciousness opens and the whole system gets physically, mentally, and spiritually elevated, your life becomes worth living.

Little things will cease to bother you. Every up and down that comes your way makes this recurrent play of life more interesting. The truth—that every moment is supportive and complementary to your growth—starts dawning on you.

5. KNOWLEDGE AND FAITH

FEBRUARY 21, 1996

OSLO, NORWAY

In science, you have knowledge first; then faith follows. For example, science encouraged chemical farming, which the world followed. With time came the understanding that this isn't healthy, and today, science values natural farming. So when the knowledge changed, the faith also changed.

In spirituality, faith comes first; then knowledge follows. For example, if you practice *pranayama* (yogic breathing exercises) with faith that it will work, you gain an understanding of *prana* (life force). Similarly, the regular practice of meditation gives you the knowledge of consciousness. Even an uneducated person, through faith, can attain deep knowledge.

Science regards life as matter; spirituality regards even matter as life.

NEWS FLASH:

Gurudev celebrated Shivaratri, an ancient Vedic holiday celebrating meditation, at the German Academy. Volunteers put their hearts and souls into making the place beautiful. The meditations and satsang were deeply uplifting, and as usual, laughter filled the corridors of the new academy. To the surprise of everyone, the big hall is already too small.

6. YOU AND OWNERSHIP

SEPTEMBER 13, 2001

BANGALORE ASHRAM, INDIA

Mankind has a tendency to own things. When you own something small, your mind stays small; your life gets stifled, and your whole consciousness is immersed in your house, car, spouse, children, and so on.

A monk or nun leaves home and goes far away. There they also start owning their rosary, books, concepts, and knowledge. Owning has simply shifted from objects and people to ideas and practices.

But the wise know that they own the sun, the moon, the stars, the air, all of space, the entire humanity, and the Divine in its entirety. When you own something big, your consciousness also expands, and when you own something small, then small negative emotions start coming up, such as anger and greed.

I wonder why people don't feel connected to the sun? The very existence of life depends upon the sun. Perhaps it's lack of awareness that causes people to refuse to acknowledge and own their connectedness to the macrocosmic universe.

The *rishis* in ancient India, the Native Americans, and the Indigenous people from all over the globe have insisted that you can feel connected to the sun, the moon, and the directions.

When you own something vast, your consciousness also becomes vast.

NEWS FLASH:

Representatives of the Art of Living from the United States, Germany, and South Africa participated in the UN Conference on Racism in Durban. Art of Living also provided the chairperson to lead the conference and the educator caucus.

7. THREE TYPES OF DISPASSION (CENTEREDNESS)
MAY 26, 2002
JAKARTA, JAVA, INDONESIA

There are three types of dispassion:

- The first type is the dispassion that arises when you realize the misery in the world, and you fear misery. The events in life—the pain and suffering you experience or see—bring dispassion.

- The second type of dispassion is born out of your desire to achieve something higher. Some consider dispassion as a path to enlightenment. You renounce something here to gain something out there. You engage in austerities and take vows to have a better place in the afterlife.

- The third type of dispassion comes from wisdom or knowledge. A broader understanding of the transient nature of things cultures a state of nonattachment to events, objects, people, or situations, which lets you remain calm and unperturbed.

In Divine love, dispassion doesn't manifest. The attainment of this love brings such bliss and such intoxication that it not only takes away your passion but your dispassion as well.

8. WHAT IS ENLIGHTENMENT?

What is enlightenment? It's being happy unconditionally.

There are two steps to enlightenment:

1.   From being somebody to being nobody
2.   From being nobody to being everybody

And how to be nobody? Just wake up and realize the vastness of the universe. What are you in this vastness?

You may be a great businessman, a scientist, or a doctor, but how long will you be here on this planet? In seventy to one hundred years, you'll go, and the earth will continue to exist. It's been here for billions of years, and it will continue to be. Who are you? Where are you in the vast expanse of the universe?

The whole journey of life is from being somebody to becoming nobody, and from being nobody to be a part of everybody.

9. FREE FROM THE GRIP OF THE MIND

Broaden your vision. Life is much bigger than the small events that take place in life.

The mind is a wave in the ocean of consciousness.

The first step toward being free from the grip of the mind is to know that you're not just the mind. Our little mind isn't a separate entity. It has no existence of its own. It's part of consciousness.

The second stage is realizing that the mind is gripping you.

The third stage is being a witness, neither trying to get out of it nor trying to indulge in it. Observe all the events in life and everything happening inside your body as a witness. Witnessing means not participating, but just observing what is happening. Taking things *as they are* helps you to be a witness. Then you find that things are simply happening. Thoughts hover around, ideas may come and go, but you know that you're not that.

If you stand near a highway and watch all the cars pass by, or if you sit in a cafe and watch everyone eating, that's being a witness. Similarly, you already witness many thoughts that arise in your mind. You don't participate in all the thoughts. Otherwise, you'd go crazy. When you see yourself as a witness, separate from ego; then no person or situation can shake you.

Reaching this state takes time—it takes time for restlessness and the heat of desires to settle down. The greater the steadiness in being a witness, the greater the joy that springs from within.

> *Life is like a river, ever changing.*
> *Events are like the ripples, unceasing.*
> *Wisdom is like the undercurrent, silent yet strong.*
> *Self is like the riverbed, a witness to all.*

10. SPIRITUAL EDUCATION

OCTOBER 22, 1995
ADDRESS AT THE FIFTIETH ANNIVERSARY
CELEBRATIONS OF THE UNITED NATIONS
NEW YORK, NEW YORK, UNITED STATES

Spiritual education is needed to uncover the knowledge that we are, first, a part of the Divine, and, second, human beings.

In this age, even when technology has advanced so far, we have cared very little for the emotional and spiritual needs of people. Neither at home nor in school have we been taught how to release negative emotions. Either we regret the past and worry about the future or we get stuck in negativity.

A stress-free mind and disease-free body are the birthrights of every human being. Only true spiritual knowledge can help us handle our mind and bring it back to the present moment.

Breathing techniques, meditation, and yoga can be used as powerful tools to release tensions and negative emotions, enabling one to live more fully in the present moment.

11. VIRTUES

JULY 19, 2000

LAKE TAHOE, CALIFORNIA, UNITED STATES

Virtues can't be cultivated. You have to assume that they're there.

When you think you don't have a virtue, then you come from a space of lack or deficiency. If you think you don't have virtues and then try to cultivate them, you'll fail. Seekers should remember that they're born with virtues; otherwise they couldn't have been seekers.

You often compare yourself with others on the basis of virtues. Don't compare yourself with them. Simply recognize all the virtues you appreciate in others and realize that they're already present in you in seed form. You only have to nurture them.

NEWS FLASH:

The Guru Purnima celebrations started with the beautiful sound of a ceremony of gratitude being sung by hundreds of people from all over the world who traveled there to be in the presence of their spiritual teacher. The next evening, everyone gathered around Gurudev for a cruise to the middle of Lake Tahoe for a celebration of music and deep silent meditation as the full moon rose over the surrounding peaks of the Sierra Nevada Mountains of eastern California.

12. *VIVEK:* THE AWARENESS OF CHANGE

APRIL 10, 1996

JAKARTA, INDONESIA

What is *vivek*? *Vivek* is the awareness that everything is changing.

Time and again, you have to reawaken to this—that the world, people, our bodies, and our emotions are all constantly changing.

When you experience sorrow, understand that *vivek* has been overshadowed.

Question: What am I here for?

Gurudev: Be clear what you are *not* here for:

1. You are not here to blame.

2. You are not here to cry.

3. You are not here to sleep.

4. You are not here to show off.

5. You are not here to fight.

6. You are not here to be miserable.

7. You are not here to be angry.

8. You are not here to worry.

13. THE "SOLAR" PLEXUS

JANUARY 8, 1997
GERMAN ACADEMY, BAD ANTOGAST, GERMANY

The solar plexus is connected with the sun—that's why it's called solar plexus. When the first rays of the sun fall on the solar plexus, it's very good for your body. That's why it's good to do the set of yoga postures called sun salutations in the early morning.

The solar plexus has a profound impact on the central nervous system, optic nerves, stomach, and what we usually call our "gut feeling." It's the second brain in your body.

Usually, the solar plexus is slightly bigger than an almond. With the practice of yoga asanas, meditation, and SKY breathing, the solar plexus can become as large as an apricot—it then performs better and balances the bodily functions.

> *When the solar plexus contracts, one feels sad, depressed; all the negative feelings arise.*
> *When the solar plexus expands, the intuitive mind awakens; the mind becomes clear and focused.*

These days, the solar plexus remains small, but the tummy keeps getting bigger. (*Laughter*)

14. THE VALUE OF CHANTING

MAY 14, 1998

BANGALORE ASHRAM, INDIA

Your whole body is made up of atoms. Being with this truth kindles the energy in you and raises your consciousness.

When you chant or sing *bhajans* (devotional songs), the vibration of sound energy gets absorbed into every atom of your body. Your entire body gets soaked in energy and transformation happens.

A microphone absorbs sound and converts it into electricity; the body absorbs sound vibration and converts it into consciousness.

If you sit and listen to gossip or violent music, that energy gets absorbed by your body and does not leave you with a good feeling.

> *When you hear knowledge or chant with all your heart, that elevates your consciousness.*

An ancient proverb in Sanskrit says that the words of *rishis* (sages) and enlightened ones are translated into experience immediately.

15. EVERYBODY HAS THE RIGHT TO BE IMPERFECT

OCTOBER 22, 1995

UNITED NATIONS, NEW YORK, NEW YORK

Everybody has the right to be imperfect. Rather than expecting perfection in people, situations, or yourself, change your perception. The mere recognition that "this is how the world is" brings acceptance, and you become centered and calm.

16. ON SELF-ACCEPTANCE

2021

BANGALORE ASHRAM, INDIA

Your race to improve yourself is your problem. Why do you have to improve yourself? Why don't you accept yourself as you are?

When we see others, we want to be better than them. This idealizing in the mind puts you at a disadvantage. The moment you drop all your comparing and say, "I just accept myself or my situation as it is," something happens inside of you. Then you're in a state of total contentment. From there, talents that are hidden in you start to manifest.

And even if they don't manifest, you don't care. You're simply happy. When a candle glows, there's no question of half glow, less glow, or more glow. A candle glows, and that's all. It spreads its radiance all around.

That's what we must remember: that each one of us is a glowing light.

This doesn't mean that you ignore input from others. Otherwise, this can lead to arrogance. How can you avoid arrogance? Remember simplicity and be open to any type of criticism, without needing to justify, resist, or defend yourself.

17. CHANGE AND LOVE

JULY 8, 1999
MONTREAL ASHRAM, CANADA

There are some who are longing for change. Feeling that everything is stagnant in their lives, they want to change partners, careers, and homes. And there are some who are scared of change. They feel secure the way they are.

There are some who see the change, but don't acknowledge it out of fear. There are some who don't notice change at all. There are others who don't think there's anything to change.

And there are those who realize that everything is changing yet see that there's something that's non-changing. Those who recognize the non-changing amidst the change are the wisest of all.

> *Question*: Must love always change as well?
>
> *Gurudev*: The expression of love changes, but love itself doesn't change. The mother has total love for the child, but sometimes she feeds the child; sometimes she's strict with the child, saying, "Come on, sit and write!" Sometimes she disciplines the child. She does this out of love, and these are all different modes of love. So the expression of love changes. But love itself does not change, because love is your nature.

NEWS FLASH:

Canadian Broadcasting Company crews followed Gurudev around for two days and taped a high-energy satsang to be broadcast on national television.

18. THE FIVE INSIGHTS

SEPTEMBER 17, 1997

BANGALORE ASHRAM, INDIA

Love is your nature. Yet, when love finds an expression, you often get caught up in the object; your sight is caught outside. To return to your nature, you need insight.

Pain is the first insight. It takes you away from the object and turns you toward your body and mind.

Energy is the second insight. A bolt of energy brings you back to your Self.

Divine love is the third insight. A glimpse makes you so complete and overrules all relative pleasures.

Ecstasy is the fourth insight. An elevation of consciousness along with partial awareness of physical reality is bliss.

Non-dual awareness is the fifth insight—the realization that all is made up of one and only one.

> *When love glows, it's bliss.*
> *When love flows, it's compassion.*
> *When love blows, it's anger.*
> *When love ferments, it's jealousy.*
> *When love is all "no's," it's hatred.*
> *When love acts, it's perfection.*
> *When love knows, it's Divine!*

19. ENLIGHTENMENT IS LIKE A JOKE

Enlightenment is like a joke! It's like a fish searching for the ocean.

Enlightenment is the very core of our being—going into the core of our Self and living our life from there.

We all came into this world gifted with innocence, but gradually, as we became more intelligent, we lost our innocence.

We were born with silence, and as we grew up, we lost the silence and were filled with words.

We lived in our hearts, and as time passed, we moved into our heads.

Now, the reversal of this journey is enlightenment. It's the journey from the head back to the heart, from words back to silence; it's getting back to our innocence in spite of our intelligence. Although very simple, this is a great achievement.

Enlightenment is that state of being that's so mature and unshakable by any circumstance. Come what may, nothing can rob the smile from your heart. Not identifying with limited boundaries and feeling "all that exists in this universe belongs to me," this is enlightenment.

Whenever someone is ordinary, simple, innocent, and natural, that's enlightenment. Enlightenment is your very nature. It's in you already, in seed form.

When you drop all the tensions and hang-ups and become natural, then it's right in your hand. We simply need to let go of the old patterns that are in the mind, just drop them. Then you see that something in you flowers and dawns.

Enlightenment is unveiling one's own nature rather than achieving something through effort or skill.

20. A DEEP REST

MAY 6, 1999
BOSTON, MASSACHUSETTS, UNITED STATES

You can't rest when you have to do something that you can't do. And you can't rest when you feel you have to be someone you're not.

You're not required to do what you can't do. You won't be asked to give what you can't give. Nothing is expected of you that you can't provide.

Doing service involves doing what you can do. And no one wants you to be someone you're not. This realization brings you deep rest.

You can't rest if you're either over-ambitious or lethargic. Both are opposed to good rest. A lazy person will toss and turn at night and be "rest-less," and an over-ambitious person will burn inside.

Even a slight feeling that the Divine is with you brings deep rest. And prayer, love, and meditation are all flavors of deep rest. This rest brings you closer to your nature and allows your talents to manifest.

21. SACREDNESS AND YOU

DECEMBER 1, 2000

EUROPEAN ASHRAM, GERMANY

Throughout the ages in all cultures, certain symbols, places, times, and people were considered sacred. Whenever you regard a symbol, place, time, person, or act as sacred, your attention is undivided and whole.

When things are ordinary and the same, you tend to slip into unawareness and inertia. The moment you consider something sacred, your inertia disappears, and you become more alive. There is nothing as fulfilling as a sacred act. You put your heart and soul into it.

When every action of yours becomes sacred, you've become one with the Divine. Then every minute of your life, every act of yours, every place you go is sacred, and every person you meet is only your reflection.

> *Question*: Why does an act when performed repeatedly lose its sacredness?
>
> *Gurudev*: This happens when your memory overpowers your consciousness and you lose your sensitivity. For example, people living in a holy site might not feel that it's as sacred as those who come there as pilgrims. That sensitivity may not be there.
>
> *Question*: How can we preserve that feeling of sacredness in our acts?
>
> *Gurudev*: Through living in the present moment and through *sadhana* (spiritual practices). Your *sadhana* won't allow your memory to overpower consciousness. Then repetition isn't a hindrance.

It's good to feel that some symbols, places, time, and people are sacred, so you remain awake and alive.

The Native Americans consider the earth, sun, moon, and all the directions as sacred. In the Indian tradition, rivers, mountains, trees, herbs, and even animals are all considered sacred. And people? They're definitely sacred!

Various traditions honor certain people, symbols, and places as sacred. For example, the cross, Jerusalem, Christmas, and the pope in Christianity; the crescent moon, Mecca, and the month of Ramadan in Islam; and the

River Ganges, the Himalayas, and the swamis in Hinduism—all are considered sacred.

Eventually, you need to transcend and feel that the entire creation and your whole life is sacred. For the person of God, the whole world with all its symbols, places, and people is sacred at all times.

22. BOOSTING YOUR LIFE FORCE

OCTOBER 7, 1998
LONAY, LAKE GENEVA, SWITZERLAND

Heightened awareness brings you closer to reality. To realize that everything is "a happening" (rather than the result of individual action), you need higher levels of *prana* (life force).

Prana can be increased through:

1.　Fasting, fresh food

2.　*Pranayama*, SKY breathing, and meditation

3.　Silence

4.　Cold water baths

5.　Emotional peaks (Any emotion taken to its peak—sadness, happiness, even anger—flips you over and brings you more *prana*.)

6.　Presence of the spiritual teacher

7.　Singing or chanting

8.　Giving without givership, serving without doership or ego

All of these create energy, and energy elevates the consciousness and awareness.

NEWS FLASH:

Gurudev inaugurated the Women's Empowerment Camp. More than nine hundred women participated in that camp.

23. STRANGE ARE THE WAYS OF *KARMA*

APRIL 24, 1996
BANGALORE ASHRAM, INDIA

Strange are the ways of *karma* (the consequences of past actions). The more you understand, the more amazed you become.

Karma brings people together and separates them. It causes some to be weak and some to be strong. It makes some rich and some poor. All the struggle in the world, whatever there may be, is the bondage of *karma*. Its ways cut across all logic and reasoning. This understanding lifts you up and keeps you from getting stuck to events or personalities, which in turn helps you in your journey to the Self.

> *Question*: So a thief can say it's my *karma* to steal?
>
> *Gurudev*: Yes, and then the police have the *karma* to catch him too! (*Laughter*)

Only human life has the ability to be free from *karma*, and only a small percentage of people aim to be free from it. *Karma* can't be eliminated by performing actions. Only grace—the love of the Divine, which is unconditional—can burn the bondage of *karma*.

NEWS FLASH:

Huge crowds welcomed Gurudev in Singapore. Chinese musicians, Indian dancers, and many dignitaries were present, including ministers and officials of Singapore and Malaysia. Many Art of Living courses are now in progress, including those for the corporate sector.

24. WHY ARE WE IMPERFECT?

DECEMBER 19, 1996
BANGALORE ASHRAM, INDIA

> *Question*: Why are we imperfect?

Gurudev: So that we can grow to perfection. Life is a movement from imperfection to perfection. A seed contains the tree, but to become a tree, it must cease to be a seed. In life, you can either see imperfection at every step—or you can see a movement from one perfection to another perfection.

Wherever you put your attention, that will grow. If you put your attention on the lack of something, the lack will increase.

25. SACRIFICE

AUGUST 6, 1997
EUROPEAN ASHRAM, BAD ANTOGAST, GERMANY

Sacrifice is letting go of an attachment that gives you pleasure for something bigger that will bring good.

Sacrifice brings strength in life. Life without sacrifice is stagnant. Sacrifice gives you a quantum leap to a higher level.

Often people think sacrifice makes life dull and joyless. In fact, it's sacrifice that makes life worth living. The amount of sacrifice in your life brings out your magnanimity and helps you move out of misery.

A life without sacrifice is worth nothing. Zeal, enthusiasm, strength, and joy are all connected to sacrifice.

> *Question*: Some people say, "I have sacrificed so much," and complain.
>
> *Gurudev*: That's good. The thought of sacrifice has given them strength—to complain! This saves them from blaming themselves and becoming even more depressed.

Sacrifice never goes unrewarded. There can be no love, no wisdom, and no true joy without sacrifice.

Sacrifice makes you sacred.

NEWS FLASH:

A team of three Art of Living teachers went to facilitate the peace process between Armenia and Azerbaijan in Karabakh, conducting three courses for army officials and another series for civilians. An article in the *Moscow Times* reported that the factions had agreed to stop fighting only two weeks after the team started work there.

From the European Ashram: Imagine translations in ten languages simultaneously! Yet the course participants all speak one language—silence.

26. FAITH IS YOUR WEALTH

MAY 28, 1998

BANGALORE ASHRAM, INDIA

Faith is your wealth.

If you think your faith in God is doing a favor to God, then you're mistaken. Your faith in God or a spiritual teacher does nothing to God or the teacher.

Faith brings immediate strength. Faith brings you stability, centeredness, calmness, and love. Faith is your blessing.

If you lack faith, you'll have to pray for faith. But to pray, you need faith. It's a paradox. (*Laughter*)

People put their faith in the world, but the whole world is just a soap bubble. People have faith in themselves, but they don't know who they are. People think they have faith in God, but they do not really know who God is.

There are three types of faith:

1. Faith in yourself: Without faith in yourself, you think, *I can't do this; it is not for me; I will never be enlightened in this life.*

2. Faith in the world: You must have faith in the world, or you can't move an inch. You deposit money in the bank with faith that it will be returned. If you doubt everything, nothing will happen for you.

3. Faith in the Divine: Have faith in the Divine, and you'll evolve spiritually.

All these faiths are connected; you must have all three for each to be strong. If you start doubting in one, you'll begin to doubt everything.

Lack of faith in God, the world, or yourself brings fear. Faith makes you full—faithful.

Question: What's the difference between faith and confidence?

Gurudev: Faith is the beginning. Confidence is the result.

Faith in yourself brings freedom.
Faith in the world brings you peace of mind.
Faith in God evokes love in you.

NEWS FLASH:

Art of Living representatives were invited to the G-8 Summit reception in Birmingham, United Kingdom.

Art of Living was also represented in the World Health Organization conference in Geneva, Switzerland.

Teachers presented programs in St. Petersburg, Russia.

Art of Living programs for women in prisons have started in Bangalore.

27. IT TAKES COURAGE TO SAY, "I AM"

JULY 15, 1998
ALPINE MEADOWS, CALIFORNIA

The Divine is realized only in deep rest—not by doing.

All your spiritual doings are to help you become silent. You'll go further when you don't stop to enjoy the bliss or the peace. Otherwise cravings may arise.

If existence wants to give you peace and bliss, then fine; your true nature is bliss. But by trying to enjoy bliss, you step down from "am-ness" to "I am something": "I am peaceful," or "I am blissful." This is followed by "I am miserable."

It takes courage to simply say, "I am." Period.

"I am" is dispassion, centeredness. You can be anywhere and be dispassionate. Dispassionate centeredness brings energy, a spark. Indulgence in bliss can bring inertia. If you are dispassionate, bliss is still there.

Dispassion takes away the feeling of scarcity. Dispassion isn't due to lack; it comes from a sense of abundance. In passion, there is a sense of lack.

Whenever everything is in abundance, dispassion happens.
And when dispassion is there, everything comes in abundance.

Question: What do we do when we catch ourselves indulging in bliss?

Gurudev: Just this understanding creates a shift. There's no effort needed.

Knowledge is better than action to make you free.

28. DO IT UNTIL YOU BECOME IT!

SEPTEMBER 17, 1998

BANGALORE ASHRAM, INDIA

Virtues have to be practiced until they become your nature. Friendliness, compassion, and meditation (expanded awareness) should continue as practices until you realize they are your very nature.

The flaw in doing something as an act is that you look for a result. When it's your nature, you aren't attached to the result, and you continue doing it.

An action that arises from your nature is neither tiring nor frustrating. For example, daily routines like brushing your teeth or bathing aren't even considered actions because they're so integrated into your life. You do all this without doership (without a sense of egotism or personal achievement). When *seva* (service) is your nature, it happens without doership.

Question: When do you realize that compassion, meditation, and *seva* are your nature?

Gurudev: When you can't be without them.

The self-realized ones continue their practices just to set an example, even though for them, there's no need for any practice.

29. SKILL IN PRAISING

FEBRUARY 24, 2000
BANGALORE, INDIA

Often when you praise, you praise in comparison to someone else. In order to praise one person, you put down someone else. And at times, when you want to point out someone's mistake, you praise another person.

Some are stingy in praising, and some are shy. Some are simply not accustomed to praising, while there are others who cannot handle praise. Some praise with motive, and some praise just to elevate.

Some praise themselves in order to hide their own low self-esteem, while some expect others to praise them.

Praising is a noble quality. But don't confuse it with flattery. Often, people use flattery to get their work done, while genuine praise comes from deep appreciation.

Real praise dawns in a blossomed state of consciousness.

The praise that comes out of an elevated state of consciousness is simply its nature. Normally praise comes out of craving and pride. Praise that comes from a heightened consciousness comes out of fulfillment.

Praising can, no doubt, elevate the consciousness and bring enthusiasm and energy. At the same time, it can also bring arrogance. Praising is a skill.

When someone praises you, do you take it without shying away? Accepting praise without shyness is also a skill.

NEWS FLASH:

Adi Chunchunagiri Swamiji, one of the renowned spiritual leaders of South India, visited the ashram.

30. LEGENDS

JULY 5, 2000
MONTREAL ASHRAM, CANADA

Legendary is the love that withstands rejection. It will be free of anger and ego.

Legendary is the commitment that withstands humiliation. It will be one-pointed and will reach the goal.

Legendary is the wisdom that withstands turbulence. It will be integrated into life.

Legendary is the faith that withstands a million chances of doubt. It will bring perfection.

Legendary are the events that withstand time. They will become inspiration for millions.

NEWS FLASH:

The first Art of Living course was held in Bangladesh.

31. DIVINE LOVE AND THE COMPLAINING FACE

SEPTEMBER 21, 2000

BANGALORE ASHRAM, INDIA

How would you like to see yourself—happy and bubbling with enthusiasm or dull and difficult to please?

Sometimes you like to be pleased, appeased, and cajoled, so you put on a tough, upset face and act difficult to please. If a person has to appease and please you all the time, it's so tiring. People run away from those who keep a long face and expect to be cajoled and appeased.

Lovers often expend a lot of energy in cajoling, reducing the joy and celebration of the moment.

It's okay for you to show your upset mood or tendency once in a while, but doing it repeatedly is taxing for you and the people around you.

If you feel down, appease and please yourself. Your need to be appeased by someone else is a sign of limited consciousness. This is the root of ignorance. If you want attention, all you get is tension.

Become one whose enthusiasm never dies, come what may.

It's not possible to attain Divine love with a complaining face. The complaining face is a sign of an unaware mind. If you want to complain, complain to God or your spiritual teacher because both have their ears covered. (*Laughter*)

NEWS FLASH:

From a village near Alwar in Rajasthan, India, a nine-year-old girl, Uma, who was speech impaired from birth, started speaking after her Art of Living course. The same was reported of a twelve-year-old boy from Vallabh Vidyanagar in Gujarat.

Gurudev went to Rishikesh to inspire the 108 youth leaders who were beginning their service work for the 5H Program (Homes, Health, Hygiene, Human Values, and Harmony in Diversity).

32. WORSHIP—A SIGN OF MATURITY

JANUARY 18, 2001
EUROPEAN ASHRAM, BAD ANTOGAST, GERMANY

For a flame to rise up, you need space above it. In the same way, for a person to rise up in life, an ideal is needed, something to adore and worship. In worship, a sense of belonging, love, honor, and respect all come together.

However, without a sense of belonging, worship can bring low self-esteem. The ancient people knew this, so they insisted that people should feel a part of what they worship. They encouraged people to worship the sun, the moon, mountains, rivers, plants, animals, and people.

Worship is the culmination of love and appreciation. Worship prevents love from turning into hatred or jealousy and prevents appreciation from becoming low self-esteem. In life, if you don't adore or appreciate anything, you'll be filled with negativity. And a person who has nothing to worship or adore is sure to fall into depression.

Lack of adoration has led to many emotional, psychological, and social problems. If you have nothing to hold high in life, selfishness, arrogance, and violence are sure to follow. Adoring and honoring one another in society eliminates stress and fosters compassion and love.

Some see worshiping as an uncivilized and unintelligent thing to do; they think it arises from a slavish mentality. In fact, it's just the contrary. Worship can only happen through gratefulness and not through subservience.

Worship, in a true sense, is a sign of maturity and not of weakness.

Question: You said worship is the culmination of love. Does worship also have a culmination?

Gurudev: The culmination of worship is self-knowledge, *samadhi* (the experience of very deep rest and a sense of total peace within yourself).

NEWS FLASH:

Gurudev stopped at the European Ashram on his way to the Kumbh Mela in India, where millions come to honor the River Ganges and Mother Nature.

33. JOY AND SORROW

MAY 31, 2001

BANGALORE ASHRAM, INDIA

The inability to experience joy and sorrow is inertia.

Experiencing joy and sorrow is a trait of consciousness.

Being happy in one's own joy and sad in one's own sorrow is a trait of animals. Being happy at another's joy and saddened by another's sorrow is a trait of humans.

If you are saddened by others' sorrow, then sorrow will never come to you. If you are happy at another's joy, then joy will never leave you.

Seeing that every relative joy is also a misery is a sign of dispassion. And seeing both joy and sorrow as just a technique to evolve is a sign of intelligence.

Considering sorrow as mere illusion is wisdom.

Transcending joy and sorrow and being established in the self is perfection.

34. ENTHUSIASM AND DISPASSION

JULY 1, 2002

WASHINGTON, D.C., UNITED STATES

What is enthusiasm? Enthusiasm means being connected to God within.

When you're with your source, you can only be enthusiastic. And you can't help but be enthusiastic when your mind is totally in the present moment. Apathy is when you're away from the source of life.

Know that dispassion (centeredness) isn't apathy; it's simply a broader perspective of reality. Dispassion simply means the way back home. It's the journey toward the source, which is a reservoir of enthusiasm.

Even though dispassion and enthusiasm appear to be opposite, they're actually complementary. When they coexist, there's perennial enthusiasm and profound dispassion.

35. ENLIGHTENMENT

We think we are just this body/mind complex with a few emotions, some little thoughts, little likes and dislikes. The truth is that we are much beyond these things. Enlightenment is simply peeling off layers and becoming totally centered in the Self.

Get to that spot where you feel absolute comfort and absolute freedom. That is liberation, that is nirvana, that is self-realization, that is yoga, and that is unity. You can call it by so many names. Too much reading can confuse you about it. That's why I say, "Be natural; be simple."

> *Question*: What is enlightenment?
>
> *Gurudev*: It can't be said in words; it has to be felt. You can't describe love. You can't say that love is endorphins or oxytocin getting produced in your body; it is something that only the heart can know; your existence can feel something different.

The funniest thing is that enlightenment is in everybody; it's in the original nature of our being and everybody has it, but it hasn't been uncovered.

There are many who have this experience of enlightenment—they feel something, and it starts happening. They have the ability to love everyone and be a "nobody" (someone without identification or ego).

You don't have to label yourself "I am enlightened, I am enlightened"—not at all!

The moment you drop all that and say, "I want nothing, and I am nothing," that moment you realize that all the forms and names are nothing; they are all like waves in the ocean. The wave is nothing but the ocean.

This conviction is enlightenment. The sea is there, the sun is there, the moon is there, and like that I, too, am here . . . that is it. Going beyond time is enlightenment. Not being constrained by space is enlightenment. Realizing you are love, everything else is love—that is enlightenment. Being so natural and feeling at home with everyone because there is no other is enlightenment.

The Spiritual Teacher

1. YOUR SPIRITUAL TEACHER IS THE DOOR

JULY 12, 1995

MONTREAL ASHRAM, CANADA

Imagine you're lost on the street. There's rain, thunder, wind, and cold; you need shelter. You look around, and you see a door. You go to the door because it's more inviting, charming, and joyful than anything out on the street.

When you enter the door of your spiritual teacher, you come home. You see the world from a new perspective. From inside, you can still hear the thunder and see the rain, but it no longer disturbs you. Inside there's warmth and security. The world looks much more beautiful—not a nasty place, but a place filled with love, cooperation, and compassion. Your fear drops away.

When you can see the whole world through the eyes of your spiritual teacher, it's a sign that you've come to your spiritual teacher; you've entered the door. This is the purpose of having a spiritual teacher.

If you're still seeing the world as before, you're still standing out in the street, cold and wet; you're only looking at the door. You haven't yet entered in.

What does it mean to "see through the eyes of your spiritual teacher"? Just this: In every situation or complication that you face, you think, *How would my teacher handle it? If someone blames the teacher, what would he or she do?*

The key is to feel the presence of your teacher. Your spiritual teacher *is* the presence, not a relationship. Relationships can be broken, mended, and broken again. There's craving and aversion in every relationship. This is the wheel of *samsara* (the cycle of birth and death), the misery of the world. All relationships go topsy-turvy, whereas the presence is vast, infinite, stable, and centered.

Don't make your connection to your spiritual teacher a worldly relationship. "Oh, he looked at me." "He didn't look at me." "Oh, he said this." "He didn't say that." "Somebody else is close; I'm not close." All this is nonsense.

Just enter the door and come home. The presence will bring fulfillment to your life—and to all your relationships.

2. REASONS TO BE WITH A SPIRITUAL TEACHER

JANUARY 12, 2000

EUROPEAN ASHRAM, BAD ANTOGAST, GERMANY

These are the main reasons to be with a spiritual teacher:

1. You want to be free from misery.

2. You'd like to have your wishes fulfilled.

3. You want your talents to manifest.

4. There's a compelling urge inside you.

5. Everything else looks bleak, and there's so much joy around the teacher.

6. You want to find stability and centeredness, because those experiences happen spontaneously in the presence of the teacher.

7. You want to evolve and become enlightened; you want to attain higher knowledge.

8. You have a vision or goal that you share with the teacher, whom you see as a visionary.

9. You're there just to serve.

If you're with a spiritual teacher, it's because you belong there with the teacher. It's beyond choice.

NEWS FLASH:

The president of Italy sent a message congratulating the Art of Living Foundation for its contributions and wishing us success with our program.

3. FIVE SIGNS OF AN ENLIGHTENED MASTER

SEPTEMBER 24, 1997

BANGALORE ASHRAM, INDIA

In the presence of an enlightened master:

- Knowledge flourishes.
- Sorrow diminishes.
- Joy wells up without any reason.
- Lack diminishes; abundance dawns.
- All talents manifest.

To the degree you feel connected to an enlightened master, these qualities blossom in your life.

Sit with your eyes closed and feel your connection with the enlightened master.

NEWS FLASH:

Art of Living groups are launching service projects, including free medical aid, sanitation, and housing for the poor, and blood donation camps.

4. DIFFERENT PERSPECTIVES ON A GURU

MAY 17, 2000

TAIPEI, TAIWAN

In the East, having a spiritual master is considered a matter of pride. A master is a symbol of security, of love, and a sign of great wealth. Being with a master or guru is being with one's Higher Self. Those not having a master are looked upon as being orphaned and unfortunate.

In the West, having a master is considered a matter of shame and a sign of subjugation. Masters enforce slavery upon the weak and helpless.

In the East, people take pride in having a guru for every discipline—a religious guru (*Dharma Guru*), a family guru (*Kula Guru*), a guru for a particular discipline (*Vidya Guru*), and a spiritual guru (*Satguru*).

In the East, masters make their disciples powerful, while in the West, masters are thought to make people weak.

In the East, there's a deep sense of belongingness that enables people to dissolve their limited identity into infinity. The Saints are the most powerful and most respected because they've given up all their negativity and become one with the Divinity.

5. A WINDOW TO INFINITY

A spiritual teacher is like a window, a window to infinity. The sun shines behind the wall, as well as behind the window. But we can't see the sun behind the wall.

Through the window, you can see the sun, you can see the sky, you can see the infinite. Through a spiritual teacher, you can be connected to the infinity, to the Higher Self.

Your Higher Self:
The Divine in You

1. THE MOST BEAUTIFUL SPOT IN THE UNIVERSE

FEBRUARY 1, 1996
HONOLULU, HAWAII, UNITED STATES

There's a place you can go where everything is beautiful. Tourists travel from place to place looking for beauty. They try to take the beauty back home with them through photos and souvenirs. They only get tired and tanned.

Yet the most beautiful spot anywhere is right here. When you're in that spot, you find that wherever you are, everything is so beautiful.

> *Where is this place?*
> *Don't look here and there. Go within.*
> *When you're here, then any place is beautiful. Then wherever you go, you add beauty there.*

When you're unhappy, even the moon irritates you. Sweet things can seem nauseating, and music disturbs you. When you're calm and centered inside, noise is musical, clouds are magical, and rain is liquid sunshine.

Book yourself on a trip to this most beautiful place in the universe. Then you'll find that every day is a vacation and a celebration.

2. SILENCE

SEPTEMBER 21, 1995

BANGALORE ASHRAM, INDIA

> *Prayer within breath is silence.*
> *Love within infinity is silence.*
> *Wisdom without words is silence.*
> *Compassion without aim is silence.*
> *Action without a doer is silence.*
> *Smiling with all existence is silence.*

3. WHAT IS TRUTH?

What is Truth? That all things are changing. This will all go.

This body will change. This universe will change. These circumstances and situations will all change. People will change—their ideas and opinions will change.

What are you unhappy about? You're unhappy about situations and circumstances in your life. How long are they going to be there? Not forever. They all move and change.

Or you're unhappy about the people around you. Are they going to be there forever? They're moving and changing. It's all like a flowing river. Wake up and see that the person you saw last night is not the same person this morning. They are like bubbles on the surface of water, fleeting and changing.

Are you unhappy about the health of your body? Even if it's very healthy, how long can you hold on to your body? One day it's going to drop. If the body gets sick, attend to it. That's enough. It's the nature of the body to be sick and healthy.

From pleasant to unpleasant, and from unpleasant to pleasant, these cycles continue. This is truth. Yet something in you is untouched by time. Time comes and goes, but something in you stays forever. Changes happen in the body, but you go on forever.

Imagine that you're standing on the beach, and a wave comes and surges over your feet. When the wave recedes, it takes some mud from under your feet, but nothing happens to your feet. The same thing happens with time.

Time flows through, takes some mud from under your feet, and goes away. It can't do any harm to you.

Reminding yourself of this is truth.

4. LIGHT OF THE CREATOR

OCTOBER 17, 1995

HALIFAX, NOVA SCOTIA, CANADA

There are two kinds of people in the world. Those who think that all people are intrinsically bad, and those who think that deep inside everyone is good. The latter know that even if someone's behavior is a little questionable, it is only at the circumference.

The first kind of people can't trust anybody, and the second tend to not doubt too much.

The world becomes the way we perceive it. If you see the world as full of horrible people, then those types of situations and people will manifest in front of you. If you see the world as full of good people, you'll find goodness deep inside even the worst criminal.

There is no bad human being. Everyone has the light of the Creator in them. Many times the light is partially visible or even hidden, and sometimes it is bright and glowing.

5. SELF

MAY 16, 1996

BANGALORE ASHRAM, INDIA

Often people think of the Self as the mind-body complex. This is an erroneous notion. Neither the body nor the mind is the Self. All the yoga you do is for the body. All the meditation you do is for the mind.

Whether calm or disturbed, your mind remains the mind.

Whether sick or well, your body remains the body.

Self is all-encompassing. Service without ego, love without reason, knowledge without intellect, life beyond time and events—these are what you are.

The only purpose for this body to exist is to make you aware of how beautiful you are. And to make you aware that it's possible to live all the values you cherish and create a world of Divinity around you.

NEWS FLASH:

Tents were pitched to house a thousand guests who came from all over for Gurudev's fortieth birthday celebration. Ancient Vedic chants enlivened the morning air. In the evening, everyone danced with candles in their hands, which made the amphitheater where he spoke look like a festive cake.

6. HOW TO GET CENTERED

SEPTEMBER 10, 1997
BANGALORE ASHRAM, INDIA

Shift your awareness from the experience to the experiencer. All experiences are on the circumference; they keep on changing. The unchanging experiencer is at the center. Again and again, come back to the experiencer.

If you're frustrated, instead of spending all your time on the experience of frustration, ask, "Who is frustrated?"

If you're unhappy, ask, "Who is unhappy?"

If you think you know something, ask, "Who knows?" (*Laughter*)

If you think you're enlightened, ask, "Who is it that's enlightened?"

If you think you're ignorant, ask, "Who is ignorant?"

If you think, "Poor me," ask, "Who is 'poor me'?"

If you think you're highly devoted, ask, "Who's devoted?"

Shed all your faces and face the "I."

NEWS FLASH:

In Pune, the chief minister of Maharashtra conferred an award upon Gurudev for outstanding contribution to humanity.

7. INSIDE OUT

MARCH 19, 1998

RISHIKESH, INDIA

Often people say, "Be the same on the outside as what you are on the inside." I ask you, how is this possible?

Inside you are a vast ocean, an infinite sky. Outside you are finite—just a small, limited form, a normal, changeable person!

All that you are inside—the love, the beauty, the compassion, the Divinity—doesn't show up fully outside. Only the surface layer of behavior shows.

Ask yourself, "Am I really my behavioral patterns? Am I really this limited body-mind complex?" No, you aren't the same inside as outside.

> *Don't mistake the outer layer for who you are inside.*
> *And don't show your infinite Self outside, for infinity is not easily understood.*
> *Let there be some mystery.*

8. EXPANSION OF CONSCIOUSNESS IS PEACE AND JOY

AUGUST 26, 1998

HAMBURG, GERMANY

When consciousness moves through the body in limited channels, pleasure is experienced. But repeated enjoyment of sensory stimuli causes inertia and dullness. Often cooks don't enjoy their own food. The same piece of music heard over and over loses its charm. People in the sex industry don't enjoy sex.

If you consciously observe your own experience of sensory stimuli, then consciousness expands and becomes peace. With awareness, these stimuli lose their significance. When the sun is shining, it makes no difference whether or not the candle is lit. The realization that all pleasures are just stimuli, and that you are much more than the stimuli, brings freedom.

When consciousness shrinks, the sensation of pain and suffering arises. Pain is nothing but consciousness wanting to expand and to become free. Pain is not a permanent state. Freedom is liberation from craving or sensory stimuli.

Moving toward joy is the natural tendency of life. Joy is your true nature.

Intellectual stimuli and freedom bring a joy that is longer lasting than the joy of sensory stimuli.

Like the insomniac who's forgotten how to sleep, most of us have forgotten how to be at peace and in bliss.

Like the natural tendency of air, which is to not be under pressure, and the natural tendency of water, which is to flow downward, the natural tendency of consciousness is to expand and be at peace.

> *Question*: What about the pleasure we experience in satsang?
>
> *Gurudev*: The pleasure of satsang takes you toward expansion.

The nature of expanded consciousness is not just peace; it's also joy.

NEWS FLASH:

Gurudev visited Finland for the first time, staying for a total of fifteen hours. In this short time, he made the headline news on the main television channel.

In Hamburg, Gurudev addressed the oldest Rotary Club of Europe and held a beautiful satsang in a fully packed church, where he was warmly welcomed by the parish priest.

9. THE GOAL OF ALL ANSWERS

MARCH 16, 2000

RISHIKESH, INDIA

Some questions can only be answered in silence. Silence is the goal of all answers. If an answer doesn't silence the mind, it's no answer.

To the question "Who am I?", the only relevant answer is silence. You need to discard all answers in words, including "I am nothing," or "I am the cosmic self," or "I am the Self." Just stick to the question: "Who am I?"

When you ask the question "Who am I?" and discard the words, you get no answer—there's only silence. That's the real answer. Your soul is solidified silence, and this solidified silence is wisdom, knowledge.

All other answers are just thoughts, and thoughts can never be complete. Only silence is complete.

Thoughts aren't the goal in themselves. Their goal is silence. The easy way to silence thoughts is to arouse the feelings, for only through feelings will peace, joy, and love dawn, which are all your very nature.

10. THE "I" DOESN'T CHANGE

This universe is very dynamic. Nothing is static here. What appears to be static is an apparent illusion. Everything is moving, growing, and changing constantly. But we don't see it that way. When someone meets you after not seeing you for some time, he tells you that you have gotten fat or become thin. Otherwise, you look at your clothes and notice that your pants (or shirts) have become loose, tight, or whatever.

Change is always visible with a reference. It's because of the reference point that you're able to perceive the change. So when we see everything is changing, then there must be something that isn't changing. Otherwise, how can you see the change?

What is that something that doesn't change in you? You can't see it, but you can feel it. You have an idea, a sense, that there's something that's not changing.

You can experience that something in your body or deep inside you, what you call "I" is not changing. Everything else is changing. Thoughts are changing; ideas are changing; emotions are changing; feelings are coming and going.

The body has undergone tremendous change. The body changes so fast. Every minute new cells are being born, and old cells are dying out. Our blood is changing. All the fluids in the body change within twenty-four to forty-eight hours. Flesh, skin, and bone all change within weeks. Within three months, the bone marrow changes. The entire body, which appears to be solid, is not solid! It's changing. Then, that non-changing reference that we vaguely feel somewhere, becomes more and more clear.

11. JUST BE

JANUARY 5, 1996
WEGGIS, SWITZERLAND

True joy is going beyond your identity.
Mature love is feeling the oneness beyond emotions.

Real rest is reposing in your being.
Relax and just be!
Events are transitory.
Like a bee that sucks nectar from different flowers,
gather the nectar of wisdom from events and move on.
Be like a busy bee and be in the Being!

12. ANGELS

MARCH 5, 1997
SINGAPORE

Infinity or the Self has diverse qualities, and those qualities assume names. They're called angels.

Angels are simply rays of your "Big Self." They're like your extended arms. They're there to serve you when you're centered. Just as roots, stems, and leaves come out of a sprouted seed, all the angels in your life manifest when you're centered.

In the same way that all the colors are present in white sunlight, all the angels are present in your Higher Self. Bliss is their breath; centeredness is their abode.

Angels rejoice in your company, but you have nothing to gain from them. They only come around those who have nothing to gain from them.

13. THE EGO IS ONLY AN ATOM

JULY 30, 1998
MONTREAL ASHRAM, CANADA

The "I," or ego, in you is a tiny atom. It can either become associated with matter or with spirit. Whatever it becomes associated with, it identifies with that.

When associated with matter, it identifies with the body. When associated with Being, it identifies with the infinite Self.

When this atom, this ego, is associated with the material world, it becomes mundane. When it is associated with the spirit, it becomes spiritual, Divine. It becomes *shakti* (primordial cosmic energy) when associated with the Being, the Self. It becomes miserable when identified with the body.

In a huge atomic reactor, it is just one tiny atom that's exploded. In the same way, in our whole body, there is just one little, tiny atom of "I." And when this "I" explodes, it becomes the light of the Self.

Usually, we say, "I am miserable" or "I am happy."

Shift this atom of "I" from identifying with the body and the conceptual world to identify with the Being.

NEWS FLASH:

Gurudev's public talk on "Human Values" at the elegant Chateau Laurier in Ottawa made the TV evening news.

14. TRUTH

JUNE 15, 2000
EUROPEAN ASHRAM, BAD ANTOGAST, GERMANY

Truth is that which doesn't change. Examine your life and identify all that changes as "not Truth." With this outlook, you'll find that you're surrounded only by not-Truth (or untruth).

When you identify that which appears to you as untruth, then you will become free from it, but if you don't identify it, you can't become free.

Your own experiences in life make you identify your own untruth. As you mature in life, you find that everything is changing—events, situations, people, emotions, thoughts, opinions, concepts, and even your body. You see that everything is untruth. It's only then that satsang, which literally means "the company of truth," happens in the real sense.

For example, until the child becomes an adult, a mother can't see the child as untruth unless she steps back and sees motherhood as one of her roles. For a toddler, candy isn't untruth, and for a youth, sex isn't untruth.

> *Question*: Is knowledge also untruth?
>
> *Gurudev*: Yes, if it's words, it's untruth. But as existence, it's truth.

Love as an emotion isn't truth; as existence, it is truth.

NEWS FLASH:

After a beautiful satsang on a boat in Paris, Gurudev has arrived for a brief and busy stay at the European ashram in Bad Antogast, Germany.

The Art of Living in Shimla, India, has undertaken a "Clean Shimla" project and a polyethylene bag-free city project.

15. MORNING REFLECTIONS

(FROM GURUDEV'S COMMENTARY
ON THE ASHTAVAKRA GITA)

In the morning when you get up, feel as though you are the infinite sky.

Become aware of your nature.

What is your nature? You are the most amazing and wonderful being. Your nature is infinite and pure, full of light and love. This is what you are. The day should begin remembering and reliving this, like the sun rising. When you have risen from sleep, the sun in you has come up.

Walk in the morning, floating like a cloud, remembering your true nature.

Oneness/God/The Divine

1. SEEING GOD

MARCH 13, 1996
SWARGASHRAM (HEAVENLY RETREAT), RISHIKESH, INDIA

Meditation is seeing God in yourself.
Love is seeing God in the person next to you.
Wisdom is seeing God everywhere.

Love finds expression in service.
Joy finds expression in an undying smile.
Peace expresses itself as strength.

2. FALSE SECURITY

JANUARY 28, 1998
SANTA MONICA, CALIFORNIA, UNITED STATES

False security doesn't allow your faith to grow. Faith only grows when you've dropped your securities.

False security is keeping faith where it doesn't belong—having a job, a house, friends, etc., gives an illusion of security.

Even if you have all the material securities, without faith, you'll still reel in fear. And when you buffer your life with these securities, you keep faith away.

Faith is your greatest security. Faith brings perfection in you.

Keep money in the bank or in your pocket, not in the mind. Keep the house where it belongs, not in the mind. Keep friends and family where they belong, not in the mind.

You have to let go of all possessions in the mind.

Your body belongs to the world.
Your spirit belongs to the Divine.
The Divine is your only security.

Faith is realizing that you always get what you need.
Faith is giving the Divine a chance to act.

NEWS FLASH:

Gurudev gave a talk to more than two hundred people at the World's Great Religions and Their Transformation in the 21st Century Symposium at the University of California, Los Angeles.

3. BLESSING

MAY 13, 1999
EUROPEAN ASHRAM, BAD ANTOGAST, GERMANY

Make your home God's home, and there will be light, love, and abundance. Make your body God's abode, and there will be peace and bliss. Feel like your mind is a toy of God, and you'll watch and enjoy all its games.

See the world as a play and display of God, and you'll repose in the Self beyond duality!

Blessing comes to you in many forms:

If you're generous, blessing comes to you as abundance.
If you're hardworking, blessing comes to you as reward.
If you're pleasure-loving, blessing comes to you as dispassion (centeredness).
If you're caught up in attachments, blessing comes to you as sorrow.
If you're centered, blessing comes to you as knowledge of the Self!

NEWS FLASH:

Gurudev gave a talk at Harvard University in Boston on the topic of children, violence, and the Art of Living course for youth, a meditation program designed for elementary school students. Afterward, there was a lively satsang in the evening. Then it was on to Virginia and Washington, D.C.

In addition to the large satsangs, Gurudev also addressed doctors and scientists at the National Institutes of Health, where Dr. Janakiramaiah, who has done research on SKY Breath Meditation, presented his paper. The response was enthusiastic.

A Human Values Conference was held in which diplomats and officials from many countries participated before the American spring tour finished in Great Falls, Virginia.

The Art of Living course has been approved for the employees of the judiciary in Wayne County in Michigan, and the course for youth is in full swing in several states in the United States.

4. BE-LOVED

FEBRUARY 12, 1997

FORT LAUDERDALE, FLORIDA, UNITED STATES

When knowledge is lodged in you as wisdom, it will never leave you—wisdom lodges in your heart.

Keep your heart in a safe place. It's too delicate. Events and small things make strong impressions on it. To keep your heart safe and your mind sane, you can't find a better place than the Divine. Events and the passing of time won't be able to touch you; they won't create a scar.

A precious stone needs a setting around it to hold it. Wisdom is the setting that will hold your heart in the Divine.

Just BE . . . and know that you are loved. That is "beloved."

Make the Divine your sweet beloved. This is the last thing and the first thing to do.

NEWS FLASH:

From Los Angeles, Gurudev visited New Jersey, New York, Philadelphia, and Houston for satsangs and packed talks.

5. INTENSIFY YOUR LONGING

MAY 21, 1998
BANGALORE ASHRAM, INDIA

Union with the Divine depends on the intensity of longing and not on the time spent seeking or qualifications of the seeker.

There's an Indian proverb that says, "It may take some time to pick a flower, but it takes no time to meet the Divine!" Your abilities or qualifications aren't the criteria—it's simply the intensity of your longing.

Intensify your longing for the Divine right away. This happens when you know that you aren't just the small self and want nothing.

> *Question*: What's the difference between desire and longing?
>
> *Gurudev*: Desire is the fever of the head. Longing is the cry of the heart.

NEWS FLASH:

This week, Gurudev came up with yet another service project: Health, Hygiene, Homes, Human Values, and Harmony in Diversity—the 5H program. Immediately, inspired Art of Living practitioners took action to provide drinking water, sanitary facilities, and more than six hundred homes for the homeless in rural districts all over India.

6. BLISS

JANUARY 6, 1999
EUROPEAN ASHRAM, BAD ANTOGAST, GERMANY

All you seek in your life is bliss, that Divine union with your source. And everything else in the world distracts you from that goal. There are a zillion things to distract you from that goal in so many unexplainable, incomprehensible ways of not coming home.

The mind is kept alive by cravings and aversions, shoulds and shouldn'ts, wants and dislikes. Only when these fade and the mind dissolves does bliss dawn. Absolute bliss can't be understood.

It's extremely difficult to get into absolute bliss. After a long time—many lifetimes—you get into bliss.

Bliss is the abode of all Divinity. Only in this human body is it possible to experience and uphold it. Having a human life and access to this wisdom, if you still don't realize this, you're at the greatest loss.

There's no use in being polite only in your behavior. If you're rude in your behavior, it's acceptable, but not if you're rough in your heart.

The world doesn't care how you are inside; it only looks at your behavior. The Divine doesn't care how you are on the outside; it only looks at how you are inside.

Never let even a tiny bit of dislike or craving lodge itself in your heart. Cravings and aversions make your heart hard. Let your heart be fresh, soft, and fragrant like a rose.

It's such an illusion! You dislike someone or something, and this only makes you hard, and your hardness takes a long time to soften, to disappear. It's such a trap for keeping you away from the treasure.

Nothing in this material world can give you contentment. An outward-looking mind seeking contentment gets discontented, and the discontentment grows. Complaints and negativity start hardening the brain, clouding the awareness (the aura), and forming a huge cloud of negative energy. When the negativity reaches its peak, like an overinflated balloon, it bursts and comes back to the Divine.

You can never escape the Divine—either through the long route of negativity or the positive approach, which is instantaneous. When Divinity dawns, in no time at all the shift happens from the untruth to truth, from darkness to light, from the dull inert matter to the sparkling spirit.

NEWS FLASH:

In Poland, as the mercury dipped to -13 Fahrenheit, one hundred huge bags of warm clothes and sleeping bags were collected for the poor and homeless. It took four trucks to transport the clothes and sleeping bags to those in need.

The Polish police sent a plainclothes policeman to investigate the Art of Living courses in the city of Rzeszow. The policeman liked the course so much that he is now arranging for the whole police force in Rzeszow to do the course.

Prison courses are starting in West Bengal and Gujarat.

In Slovenia, two courses were conducted for people suffering from multiple sclerosis. Senior doctors from the Institute of the Republic of Slovenia for Rehabilitation conducted research when the course was in progress and documented good results.

7. STRETCHING THE EMPTINESS

FEBRUARY 3, 1999

BANGALORE ASHRAM, INDIA

Question: The Buddha said, "The whole world is misery, and what is to be achieved is emptiness." What is emptiness?

Gurudev: Emptiness is the doorway between the material and spiritual worlds. It's where you come to understand the nature of the spirit. From this emptiness begins the fullness.

On one side of emptiness is misery, and on the other side is bliss.

> *Stretching the Sound is Music.*
> *Stretching the Movement is Dance.*
> *Stretching the Smile is Laughter.*
> *Stretching the Time is Boredom.*
> *Stretching the Mind is Meditation.*
> *Stretching the Life is Celebration.*
> *Stretching the Devotee is God.*
> *Stretching the Feeling is Ecstasy.*
> *Stretching the Emptiness is Bliss.*

NEWS FLASH:

Clothes were distributed to about five hundred villagers as part of the service project of the Bangalore ashram.

8. THE DIVINE LOVES YOU DEARLY

I have come here only to tell you that the Divine loves you dearly.

This reminder softens you, brings about miracles around you, and changes your life.

We'll all die one day. Though we may keep all our valuables in a safe and keep the keys safely with us, when we die we'll leave both the safe and keys behind. We don't take anything with us.

When you travel in a car, do you consider that to be your home? You might enjoy it for the duration of your journey, but what would happen if you thought that was your home? Once you reach your destination, you have to get out. Once you pull into the garage, you have to get out of the car.

The ultimate truth of life is that we will leave everything behind.

The Divine loves you very deeply. It does not matter what you call this supreme power. You need not fear or worry. Live your life with a smile. I am here only to help you realize this.

9. LONGING ITSELF IS DIVINE

FEBRUARY 8, 2001
BANGALORE ASHRAM, INDIA

Longing for worldly things makes you dull. Longing for infinity fills you with life.

But longing also brings along a sense of pain. To avoid the pain, you try to push away the longing. The skill is to bear the pain of longing and move on. Don't try to find a shortcut to overcome longing. Don't make the longing short—that's why it's called *loooonging*. (*Laughter*)

True longing in itself brings up spurts of bliss. That's why in ancient times in India, longing was kept alive by singing and listening to stories about the Divine.

People often think wisdom is devoid of longing. No, such wisdom is dry. The longing that comes in true wisdom makes life juicier. The Divine is certainly juicy!

Longing gives you the power to bless. Bless the entire creation. For the longing in you itself is godliness.

NEWS FLASH:

In Kerala, Gurudev met with His Holiness Baselios Marthoma Mathews II, the sixth Catholicos of the Indian Orthodox Church and a descendant of St. Thomas. He also inaugurated homes for the elderly near Mysore.

10. THE DEVOTEE BECOMES GOD

SEPTEMBER 28, 2000

BANGALORE ASHRAM, INDIA

When a river meets the ocean, it no longer remains a river. It becomes the ocean. A drop of the ocean is part of the ocean. In the same way, the moment a devotee meets or surrenders to the Divine, the devotee becomes God.

When the river meets the ocean, it recognizes that it is the ocean from the beginning to the end. Similarly, the individual "I" dissolves in one Divinity.

Sometimes it seems that the ocean is pushing back the river. Sometimes the ocean goes into the river to greet it. Similarly, the Divine puts many questions and doubts in the mind or provides an amazing experience to bring you back home.

NEWS FLASH:

Construction activities for the large meditation hall, the big water tank, and more residential facilities are in full swing at the Bangalore Ashram to enable a greater number of retreat participants to participate in future celebrations.

11. I AM GOD

DECEMBER 10, 2000

KANNUR, KERALA, INDIA

It was thought that to say, "I am God," is blasphemy. I tell you, to say, "I am *not* God," is blasphemy. When you say, "I am not God," you deny God's omnipresence.

You are made up of love. If you say, "I am not God," you're denying that God is love, and that's blasphemy.

"I am" is your consciousness. If you say, "I am not God," you deny that God is aware, alert, and awake.

You exist. When you say, "I am not God," you deny God a portion of existence, and that is blasphemy. You're denying the scriptures that say, "God made man in His own image." If you say, "I am not God," you're denying God.

> *Question*: If God is omnipresent, why is there hatred and suffering in this world?
>
> *Gurudev*: Truth transcends duality, and God is the absolute and only truth.

In that non-changing truth, there are no opposites. All the opposites are part of the ever-changing existence, which isn't the complete picture.

Good and bad, right and wrong, everything is relative. For example, milk is good, but too much milk can harm you. A drop of poison can save a life— many medicines have "poison" written on them. They're neither absolutely good nor bad; they just are.

In a movie, when light passes through the film, it doesn't matter to the light what the film is—whether it's a tragedy, comedy, or one with a happy ending. Whether projecting a hero or villain, the light is always there.

In the same way, no matter what's happening in your mind, you are God.

NEWS FLASH:

In Kannur, a politically disturbed small town, all the different religious and political factions forgot their differences for a day and sang united and strong in a satsang of more than two hundred thousand people. Nearly one million people in Kerala participated in satsang and meditation with Gurudev over the last five days.

12. ABIDING IN THE SELF, A VALENTINE'S DAY TALK

FEBRUARY 14, 1996
LONDON, UNITED KINGDOM

Spirit and matter are made for each other. They uphold each other.

If you only hold on to matter and don't respect the spirit, then matter can't thrive. If you honor the spirit, then you'll care for the world, and when you care for the world, it'll take care of you.

> *God is the valentine of the whole world, residing in every heart. While love exists in every heart, it expresses itself in different flavors. You can't behave the same way with everyone, but you can love everyone. Recognize love beyond behavior and social norms. Abiding in the Self, you become the valentine for the whole world.*

NEWS FLASH:

The village of Upholland in Lancashire held a silent retreat led by Gurudev. Gurudev gave a talk on "Ayurveda and the Art of Living" to a packed hall at the Liverpool Medical Institution.

13. A PRAYER

APRIL 15, 1999
KAUAI, HAWAII, UNITED STATES

> *Give me not thirst if you cannot give me water.*
> *Give me not hunger if you cannot give me food.*
> *Give me not joy if I cannot share.*
> *Give me not skills if I cannot put them to good use.*
> *Give me not intelligence if I cannot perceive beyond it.*
> *Give me not knowledge if I cannot digest it.*
> *Give me not love if I cannot serve.*
> *Give me not desire that doesn't lead me to you.*
> *Give me not a path that doesn't take me home.*
> *Give me not a prayer if you don't want to hear it.*

Question: When you pray, to whom do you pray?

Gurudev: To my Self! In prayer the mind goes to its source, the Self. God, the spiritual teacher, and the Self are the same.

14. THANK SUPERFICIALLY

JULY 14, 1999

SEATTLE, WASHINGTON, UNITED STATES

> *Gurudev*: Which is better, to thank deeply or superficially?
>
> *Everyone in unison*: Deeply!
>
> *Gurudev*: No, superficially. (*Everyone is baffled*.) Thanking needs a separation. It means there are two. If you are deeply thankful, it means you deeply feel the separation. Does one hand thank the other hand?

Deep within, there's no need to thank because there's oneness—there's no "other." But superficially, you can thank. "Thanks" are like ripples on the surface of water.

When you say, "Thank you," you complete something. You're finishing a transaction, a relationship, a process. "Thank you" is like "Goodbye." You can complete all transactions at a surface level.

Thankfulness always exists in relation to something else. You give thanks for something; you don't give thanks for nothing at all. At the deepest level, thanking has no meaning.

> *Question*: So, should we thank superficially and feel deeply?
>
> *Gurudev*: Feeling is also superficial. If you think feeling is the depth, you haven't gone to the depth. Feeling is deeper than thinking, but feelings change. Whatever is the deepest does not change. So thank superficially, not from the depth. Deep thanks indicate deep separation!
>
> *Audience member*: Maybe we should say, "I thank you from the tip of my tongue!" (*Laughter*)

15. VARIETIES OF SPIRIT

JANUARY 27, 2000

DALLAS, TEXAS, UNITED STATES

Why should you think God is only one? Why can't God also be many? If God made humanity in God's own image, what image is that? African, Mongolian, Caucasian, Japanese, Filipino? Why are there so many types of people and so many varieties of things?

There isn't just one type of tree, not just one type of snake, mosquito, or vegetable. There isn't just one type of anything, so why should God be only one?

How could this consciousness that manifested this whole creation and that loves variety, be monotonous? God loves variety, so God must be infinite variety as well. God manifests in many names, forms, and varieties.

Some schools of thought don't give God the freedom to appear in many forms. They want God in one uniform!

You change your appearance to suit the occasion. When such is the case, how could you think there is no variety in the Spirit? Ancient people knew this and that's why they cognized Divinity as infinite qualities and forms. The Spirit is not dull and boring.

The Spirit that is the basis of creation is dynamic and ever-changing. God is not only one, but many!

When you accept the variety of Divinity, you cease to be a fanatic or a fundamentalist.

16. SEEING OTHERS AS YOURSELF

Some night, when you're tucked away safely in bed, bring to mind a thought that there are no people at all in this world except you. Other people are like shells floating in the ocean and your own *karma*, your past experience, is getting into those shells and reflecting back at you.

Can you watch a wrestling match on television and see both people as yourself? Can you feel, "It's my own consciousness that's acting one way in this mind and one way in that mind. In all these different minds, different roles are being played, but it's all me"?

A sparrow that looks in the window believes that there's another sparrow. It keeps hitting the window and stains the glass with its own blood. The sparrow fights with itself and dies. This is exactly what's happening in the world. If we're fighting, we're fighting with ourselves.

About the Author

GURUDEV SRI SRI RAVI SHANKAR is a renowned spiritual teacher, global humanitarian, and advocate for peace. His vision of personal and social transformation has ignited a global movement in over 180 countries.

Gurudev, born in 1956, was raised in South India where he studied classical Indian literature and received a degree in modern physics.

Since 1981, Gurudev has been teaching breath-based meditation techniques for health and well-being. The cornerstone of his courses is SKY Breath Meditation, a tool that helps people to:

- Lower stress, depression, and anxiety
- Restore deeper sleep
- Support heart health and cognitive functioning
- Find deeper joy and purpose

SKY has been independently researched in over one hundred peer-reviewed studies at institutions such as Yale, Stanford, the University of Wisconsin at Madison, and the University of Arizona, among others.

In the United States, many specialized programs have been offered including those for military veterans struggling with PTSD; students in inner-city schools; and healthcare workers during the COVID pandemic and afterward.

In addition to helping individuals find inner harmony, Gurudev has been instrumental in bringing leaders and communities together to promote peace in conflict-stricken areas such as Sri Lanka, Iraq, Venezuela, and others. Most notably, in Colombia he inspired the FARC to pursue a nonviolent path and return to peace negotiations. His trauma relief workshops have benefitted over 30,000 war-affected individuals: Syrian and Ukrainian refugees and survivors in Jordan, Lebanon, and Iraq, including thousands of Yazidis and other religious minorities who have been victims of terrorism and persecution.

His core message of a one-world family has inspired people from diverse cultures, races, and ethnic groups to come together for local and global service projects and celebrations.

Gurudev has spoken extensively around the world and been an invited presenter at the United Nations, the European Parliament, the World Economic Forum, as well as universities such as Harvard, Stanford, Yale, Georgetown, and the University of Southern California. He has received thirty-eight governmental awards, including the highest civilian honors in Colombia, Mongolia, Paraguay, and India. Twenty-one universities have awarded him honorary doctorates for his humanitarian and conflict resolution initiatives.

Today, Gurudev remains active, sharing his transformational techniques for mental health and wellness through his international travel and vibrant social media presence, along with a large, enthusiastic group of trained Art of Living teachers and volunteers. His timeless message of inspiration and peace continues to touch the lives of countless people around the world.